GRIZZLYVILLE

Jake MacDonald

GRIZZLYVILLE

ADVENTURES IN BEAR COUNTRY

HarperCollinsPublishersLtd

Grizzlyville
Copyright © 2009 by Jake MacDonald. All rights reserved.

Published by HarperCollins Publishers Ltd

First edition

HarperCollins books may be purchased for educational, business,
or sales promotional use through our Special Markets Department.

HarperCollins Publishers Ltd
2 Bloor Street East, 20th Floor
Toronto, Ontario, Canada
M4W 1A8

www.harpercollins.ca

Library and Archives Canada Cataloguing in Publication information is available

ISBN 978-1-55468-370-3

Printed and bound in the United States

RRD 9 8 7 6 5 4 3 2 1

For my sisters and brothers—
Wendy, Babe, Sally, Danny, Peter and Mary Kate.
With gratitude.

Contents

Introduction

Many years ago during boyhood trips to the Winnipeg zoo, I would look down into the "bear pit," where an old and half-bald bear walked backwards in perpetual circles, shaking his head back and forth as if in pathetic denial that life had come to this. The bear pit smelled like a sewer, and when the bear looked up at the crowd, hoping that someone would throw him a peanut, the glazed look in his eyes told you all you needed to know about the pain of being an animal.

A few years later I was on a fishing trip with my dad when I saw my first wild bear, a big black bear that emerged from the woods alongside a logging road and broke into a run when it saw our approaching car. For a moment the bear cantered down the sandy road ahead of us, just long enough to afford a first-class view of a large, powerful wild animal in its prime of life. The bear's rich ebony fur, rippling muscles and fluid gallop showed off a kind of physical ease that most humans will never know. After running down the slope of the sandy trail, the bear entered the bush and disappeared, but its image stayed with me and sparked a lifelong curiosity about bears that finally motivated me to write this book.

Allow me a few apologies and clarifications. There are many books on the market that provide good, accurate lessons about the life cycles of bears, their feeding habits, distribution and behaviour. This isn't one of them. I'm not a "bear expert," and this is not a book of information. It's a book of stories. Bears, for me, are a foil for the most important inquiry of all— the study of people, a study that is best undertaken through the art of the story. Throughout history, people have treated bears as objects of sport, food, jewellery, medicine, dream symbolism and so on. Some people are terrified of bears, and others are drawn to them. Some people think that bears are just overgrown pigs with fur, and others think they are vectors of religious experience. The many and varied stories you hear about bears usually tell you more about the storyteller than the subject. But that's as it should be. We study bears so we can learn about ourselves.

My friend Holly McNally owns and operates a chain of bookstores with her husband, Paul, and when I told her I was writing this book she said that all her curiosity about bears boils down to one burning question: "If I'm walking in the woods and I meet a bear, what should I do so it won't attack me?"

After spending much of my life in places where bears are abundant, and travelling around North America talking to all kinds of people who are renowned experts on bears, I would like to give Holly a useful answer. Unfortunately, I now know less about bears than when I started. Bears are ciphers, four-legged ink blots, and the impossibility of knowing anything definitive about them is what makes them intriguing.

That brings me to an explanation of the book's title. There are three types of bears in North America—black bears, polar bears and brown bears (commonly called "grizzlies")—and all get equal billing in the book. While doing my research, I came to think of "Grizzlyville" not just as a place where grizzlies live but as any place where bears and people cohabit in proximity, sharing the same piece of landscape but being perennially frightened of each other and separated by the impossibility of any kind of mutual understanding. We can love bears, respect them and work for their conservation, but we'll never know what bears think about us.

Last fall I went to the Assiniboine Park Zoo in Winnipeg to see what had changed in the decades since I saw my first bear there. The cramped, fetid bear pit is gone, replaced by a large open-air yard with free-form terrain, a deep swimming pool and tidbits concealed around the enclosure to encourage the bears to remain active. The zoo's curator, Bob Wrigley, is an author and wildlife scientist who typifies the new generation of thoughtful, dedicated zoo managers.

One morning at feeding time, Wrigley and I helped the bear keeper feed breakfast to Debbie, the zoo's polar bear. Debbie, at forty-two years of age, is an ursine octogenarian, the oldest captive bear in the world. Harold Masters, her large shaggy caregiver, led us into a narrow service corridor with a row of cages along one side. Without a word, Harold opened the outside door and Debbie came padding into her cell. Her downcast eyes made her appear shy as she ran her forehead back and forth along the bars. Harold then fixed up her breakfast—canned tuna, eggs, fresh raw meat, apples, green grapes and other goodies. He piled it up in teetering heaps, and when he was finished, it looked like the sort of platter you'd put together at an art gallery buffet if your date was a sasquatch. He squeezed the platter through the feed slot to Debbie, who then spent a couple of moments inspecting it, using a long claw like a forefinger to turn over every item on the tray.

"She's checking for smoked salmon," he said.

Then she began to eat, taking her time, chewing well and rolling her eyes periodically as if annoyed by the noise coming from the exercise yard. The grizzlies, her neighbours, were impatient for their turn, and the building was filled with an echoing *bang, bang* as they slammed their paws against the half-inch plate steel, the racket sounding like a pair of bikers kicking the door.

After Debbie finished eating, Harold filled a large squeeze bottle with Ensure, the food supplement, and squirted the chocolate-coloured liquid into her wide-open jaws. "She loves the stuff," he said.

"Is she smart?"

He paused. "I think so." Like most people who have spent their lives with bears, he seemed reluctant to make pronouncements.

"Have you ever been in the cage with her?"

"I love this bear," he replied. "And I think she likes me. We know each other really well. I've been taking care of her for fifteen years. One day she'll die, and it'll break my heart. But I would never, under any circumstances, go in the cage with her."

"Would she attack you?"

"Who's to know what she would do? She's a polar bear."

If the book raises more questions than it answers, that's why. If you're interested in learning what to do in the unlikely event of a bear attack, the best advice I heard was from an old-timer in coastal British Columbia: "You can't outrun a bear, so forget that. Just outrun the person you're with."

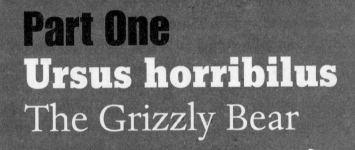

Part One
Ursus horribilus
The Grizzly Bear

If You Go
Down to the Woods

When I was a young man I had a summer job at the station operations warehouse at our local airport. We received freight from various locations and sent it off to various other locations. Then, as now, civil aviation was divided into two major civilizations. By day, passenger planes dominated the air lanes and the airports thronged with people. But the last airliners discharged their passengers around 11 p.m., and from then on, the airport emptied out and the big freighters owned the night.

From dusk until dawn my fellow employees and I sorted and dispatched all those arcane objects that soar six miles over your bed while you sleep. Plasma, gold bullion, X-ray machines, vials of swine semen, refrigerated human kidneys, mail pouches and

living creatures like goldfish, lobsters and thousands of white laboratory mice in perforated cardboard boxes. (These boxes smelled
so foul you had to hold your breath and carry them at arm's length.)
We also shipped an occasional human body. One night I loaded an
aluminum coffin onto my little tractor and pulled it up the ramp
to the turbo-prop that would carry the deceased back to his home
in Edmonton. Before we loaded the coffin onto the plane, the cus-
toms agent opened the coffin to ensure that it indeed contained a
corpse and not contraband. I snuck a glimpse, of course, and saw
a young black man in a dress green United States Army uniform.
His square-shouldered and handsome appearance suggested that
the army knew its embalming. The Vietnam War was running
wide open, and I wondered if he was one of those young men
who'd joined the army as a way of expanding his horizons. I had
once flirted with the idea of joining the Canadian air force myself,
thinking it would enable me to get a commercial flying licence
and break out of the routine of school and home life. But a couple
of my friends had gone that route and it hadn't worked out well.
So, during those long tedious nights at the warehouse, I sorted
boxes, filled out forms and wondered what a guy could do to get
himself a little adventure in this world.

As part of my job, I was required to use a foreign lexicon of
acronyms and codes. In order to save airline officials the mental
stress of having to repeat words like "Vancouver" and "Detroit"
all day long, the bureaucrats have devised a list of city codes,
each consisting of three letters. Chicago is ORD, Minneapolis is
MSP, Montreal is YUL, and so on. When a load of freight came
trundling into the warehouse, we were supposed to stack each
item on a wagon earmarked for the appropriate destination. At
three o'clock in the morning this seemed an endless and mind-

numbing job, and the codes were sufficiently nonsensical to allow for the quiet, grudging conviction that one city was the same as any other. What difference did it make, after all, if a cardboard box stuffed with serial-numbered fuel injector parts went to YQT or YQR? Most of the people who worked at the warehouse were, like me, shiftless university students who considered this kind of work to be existentially meaningless. We tried to break the monotony by shouting jokes or declaiming lines of current songs. But the common opinion was that our main task was to get all this crap loaded on a wagon and get it out of the warehouse. More than once, our crew made mistakes, dispatching a planeload of human blood or cancelled money orders to the west coast instead of the east coast, and vice versa.

So management wasn't too pleased with us. And our foreman, a bad-tempered redhead named Mr. Bomber, often paced the warehouse floor with clenched fists and bloodshot face, looking, to our delight, as if he was about to blow an aneurysm. Given the troubled mood at my workplace, I probably shouldn't have stolen a chicken. But it seemed like a good idea at the time. Our forklift driver, who was always yodelling rhymes about his baby and her proclivity for doing the hanky-panky, sometimes swept into the sorting room with a pallet load of low, flat cardboard crates. Each crate contained hundreds of baby chickens. And it was pleasant to pop open the lid and observe the little fellers, each one as yellow as a dandelion, scrambling around and tumbling over the others in a frantic attempt to take cover. The boxes were bedded with shredded floss, and there were always a few dead chicks lying feet-up in the bedding. Where were all these little chickens going? I didn't know—probably to some gigantic factory barn in YXE or someplace where they would be poured into little wire pens and stuffed with food pellets. Each chicken had a statistically nonexistent chance of escaping the meat chain, so I felt obliged to give one of them a free throw. One night, when Mr. Bomber wasn't looking, I reached into one of the crates, opened my hand, and somewhere inside the seething darkness a warm little fluffball jumped into my palm. I walked down to the end of the warehouse and put him in my locker, and at eight o'clock in the morning, I walked home with a baby chicken cheeping loudly inside my lunch pail.

When I got home, the young bird, who had by now acquired the name of Leonard, strutted about on the linoleum floor of the kitchen and sipped water from a saucer, lifting his beak in a charming birdlike way to swallow. Our family dog, Daisy, observed the newcomer with cocked head, seemingly as amused as I was. After propping small sheets of plywood across each door, I put out sufficient water and bread crumbs to keep Leonard satiated, then went to bed for a few hours. My plan was to use the afternoon to build a kind of miniature doghouse in the backyard to provide Leonard with a home. When he became large enough to fend for himself, I envisioned an arrangement in which he would roam the backyard, pecking at earthworms and settling into life as a low-ranking member of our family. I had always liked animals. When I was younger, I often kept garter snakes and turtles in the backyard, and I didn't see how my mother could object to a creature as innocuous as a chicken. But around noon, those plans all went awry when the insistent ringing of the telephone awakened me from a deep sleep.

Standing in my underwear at the hallway phone, I groggily apprehended two pieces of news. One, I was fired. The man on the phone, my shop superintendent, briskly informed me that someone had heard Leonard chirping inside my locker, and the company had no tolerance for theft. Second, I observed that Leonard was no longer with us. The sheets of plywood had been knocked over, and Daisy, who was asleep in a patch of sunlight by the living room window, had a telltale wisp of downy feather adhering to her upper lip. Opening the fridge door, I guzzled a long, thoughtful draft of milk and pondered these developments. Getting fired was indeed a complication, but being a typical twenty-year-old, I was inclined to self-justification and couldn't see how any parents could fault their son for having been the victim of a workplace layoff. These things happen all the time in the world of freight forwarding. I was more worried about the sudden prospect of time off. There were still three weeks left in August. I had managed to stash most of my salary in the bank, and the real problem, as far as I could see, was devising the best scheme for enjoying the rest of the summer.

It seemed clear that in order to make the best use of this windfall, I would need a vehicle. I belonged to a large family (seven kids), so there was a lot of demand for the family car. My father had control of the keys. My mother had secondary claim, and the kids had diminishing rights according to their age. Being fourth in line, I had slim pickings. When I did manage to get the Buick, I often brought it home with an empty tank and a new scratch on the fender. ("Dad, honestly, someone must have backed into it.") So it normally required a daylong public relations campaign to get the keys once a week. In those days, you could buy an old van for a couple of hundred dollars. Kids would take an old delivery van and strip the inside and turn it into a sort of cheap crash pad on wheels. You saw them cruising around town with curtains on the windows and bumper stickers with slogans like, "If the van is rocking, then don't be knocking!" After a few days of searching, I found a lime-green 1967 GMC Handi-Van for four hundred dollars. It had been used to deliver auto parts, and its windowless, well-beaten interior was as cavernous and musty-smelling as a steel dumpster. But I scrubbed it out with high-powered soap, glued shag carpeting to the roof and floor, attached faux mahogany panelling to the walls, built a bunk along one side and cupboards along the other, mounted some good speakers in the corners, and within a week I had created quite an attractive mobile home. My friend Dave Findlay was likewise at loose ends for the rest of the summer, and after a five-minute conversation we agreed to hit the road.

We didn't discuss where we were going; it was just assumed we would head west. In my part of the country, any young person who shakes loose automatically rolls west like a marble. If we'd thought about it, we probably would have expressed an opinion that the eastern half of the country, with its ivied downtowns and quasi-European traditions, is all about civilized society, and we wanted to go as far away from civilization as possible. We wanted to catch some fish and do some camping and maybe see a grizzly bear. So the west it was, but we were in no hurry about getting there. Our trip to the mountains was like planning a big meal in which you want to devote proper attention to the appetizers. For the first few days, we moseyed west across the prairie, taking the back roads, searching for abandoned old cars and photographing the sad, leaning, vacant-eyed farmhouses. We found one perfect ghost house that overlooked a tawny valley. Out behind the house, amongst the hip-high weeds, we found a sleeping 1940 Packard with no body damage and a forty-foot-high poplar tree growing up through its engine compartment. In the long summer twilight, we hiked riverbanks where bones of buffalo protruded from the cutbanks. We pitched tents in desolate valleys and cooked beef stew on an open fire. One evening, just as dusk was falling on the valley, an enormous full moon rose like a Chinese lantern above the hills, and as soon as it appeared a choir of coyotes began singing. They say that animals don't appreciate beauty, but how do they know? In Mexico I once saw a burro watching a sunset.

The next day at high noon, we pulled into a small prairie town and parked in front of a Laundromat. Another vehicle wheeled up behind ours and parked right up against my bumper. It was likewise a van, but it had red lights on the roof. Two Royal Canadian Mounted Policemen jumped out. They weren't much older than us.

"Hi fellas," said one of the cops. "How are you today?"

"Just fine," I replied.

"Nice van."

"Thanks."

"You got a licence?"

I gave him my licence.

"You got any registration?"

I gave it to him.

"You got any marijuana?"

"Nope."

"Oh come on. Nice van like this, you must have some weed." Brushing past me, he climbed into the van and sat in the driver's seat. He opened the glove compartment and felt around under the seats. He punched the power button on the stereo. Creedence Clearwater rolled from the speakers. He nodded his head to the music as he opened the cassette cases and examined the tapes.

"Good tunes," he remarked. "But where, oh where, did you hide the dope?"

I looked at Dave. "Where did we hide the dope?"

"I can't remember."

I looked at the cop. "I think we forgot to bring the dope."

"You *forgot* it?!"

"You know what it's like. You always forget something."

"Do you mind if I search the vehicle?"

"You're already searching it."

"You don't have to be a smart ass." He and his partner rummaged through the van for a while, then lost interest and drove off. Getting spot-checked by the cops was an ordinary part of being young and driving across the country. As far as the cops were concerned, if you were of a certain age and you were driving a camper van across the country, you probably had a bag of marijuana hidden somewhere in the vehicle. It was like a game of wits, but it was more fun for them than us. They weren't the ones facing a night in jail.

So we kept rolling along. Like Buz and Tod, the characters on the old television show *Route 66,* we spread maps on the hood of the van and decided, for no particular reason, to try this route or that. Our notion was summed up by the old Spanish proverb, "It's not the inn at the end of the day, but the road." Still, it was hard not to get excited when we topped a hill one day and spied the sawblade of the Rocky Mountains on the horizon. With each hill, the mountains got closer. Then we drove in the front door of the eastern slope, and suddenly we were inside the mountains, great wide valleys sweeping away below the highway and stunning palisades overhead. That night, we camped at the end of an abandoned road in a box canyon. You were supposed to camp in legal, serviced camp-grounds, but we preferred to poke down unmarked trails and find deserted camping places like this. As my friend Steve once opined, always break the law if you can manage it. It was chilly and very dark, and we wore woollen coats and cooked our cowboy stew on the Coleman stove. We had brought along a sack of pop music, but we needed something special to capture the mood of this place, so we opened the doors of the van and played Handel's *Messiah* at a goodly volume. Dave rolled a few numbers from the baggie we kept hidden in the dome light, and as the music boomed up into the darkness, we stood by the fire and conducted the invisible choir with burning sticks.

Later on, we climbed into our pup tents and settled in for the night. It's always cold in the mountains, even in the summer-time, and I got into the sleeping bag with all my clothes on, half thinking that it would help to keep warm and half thinking that I wanted to be dressed in case a bear came into camp and I had to scramble for the safety of the truck. I could have slept inside the impregnable metal walls of the vehicle, but I'd slept in a tent all the way across the prairies, and now that we were in the moun-tains I didn't want to turn yellow. So I lay in my heavy sleeping bag listening to the sounds of the night, knowing that Dave was as uneasy as I was. His tent was set up only a few feet away from mine, and there wasn't any of our usual banter as we waited for sleep to come. The fact that neither of us had mentioned bears all night suggested that we were trying hard to avoid the subject.

The creek gurgled somewhere in the darkness, and there was just enough wind to keep the forest stirring. The big trees creaked rhythmically, and every few minutes the undergrowth rustled, a piece of wood cracked, or the flimsy wall of the tent trembled in a sudden way that suggested something was brushing against the guy ropes. Exploring the mountains had seemed like a great idea back home. But now that we were here, tenting out in this desolate creek bottom, with the faint smell of our campfire and our beef stew drifting down the canyon, I hoped we weren't going to get a closer encounter with the wilderness than we bargained for.

* * * *

In the part of the country I grew up in, there were lots of black bears but no grizzlies.

I had read quite a lot about grizzly bears, but the books presented contrary points of view. Some authors painted a picture of a majestic and sensitive beast that just wanted to be left alone. Others portrayed an ill-tempered and fearsome animal that enjoyed tearing humans apart.

The nineteenth-century author and naturalist Ernest Thompson Seton was a spirited advocate of the benign view of bears. I had read everything that Seton wrote when I was a boy, and regarded him as the man I wanted to be when I grew up. He was a sort of Jack London figure, a gifted artist and author who was born in England and moved to Canada with his family in 1866. While roaming the wooded sandhills of western Manitoba, he sketched animals in their natural habitat and researched many of his best books, including *Wild Animals I Have Known, The Trail of the Sandhill Stag* and my boyhood favourite, *Two Little Savages.* When he began achieving success and fame, he divided his time between Canada and New York City, where he socialized with Theodore Roosevelt and Mark Twain and married a wealthy feminist named Grace Gallatin. Brooding, handsome and naturally gifted as a storyteller, Seton was one of those flamboyant nineteenth-century adventurers who racked up more accomplishments in his spare time than most people manage in a lifetime. He exhibited his art in Paris galleries, travelled the international lecture circuit, wrote thousands of articles, mapped and surveyed vast sections of northern Canada and built a castle in New Mexico. When a young local hooligan vandalized his property, Seton took him under his wing, taught him about wildlife, honour and the outdoors, and the experiment worked so well that Seton used the approach to found a little outfit called the Boy Scouts of America.

Seton despised the smug assumptions of the Victorian era. He lobbied for the rights of women and North American Indians. (He was fluent in Native sign language.) But his main accomplishment was to change the way that people thought about animals. Until Seton came along, it was commonly believed that animals were brainless organisms created by God for the benefit of humans. With stories like *The Winnipeg Wolf* and *Biography of a Grizzly,* Seton introduced animals that were fully formed characters in their own right. He didn't anthropomorphize and create furry versions of human beings as did English writers like Beatrix Potter. He was a man of science who based his fictional characters on real, historical animals he had come to know personally. For example, Meteetsee Wahb, the hero of *Biography of a Grizzly,* was a gigantic male grizzly that, for many years, he tracked and observed in the mountains near his New Mexican home. The research in his stories was scrupulous (he once spent a full day counting every feather on a blackbird so he could better understand its anatomy). But his stories were subversive in that he invested his animals with "human" qualities like affection, fear, courage and the awareness of sorrow.

In the introduction to *Wild Animals I Have Known,* he explained what a lifetime in the woods, fields and mountains had taught him about nature:

> The fact that these stories are true is the reason why all are tragic. The life of a wild animal always has a tragic end. I hope some will herein find emphasized a moral as old as Scripture—we and the beasts are kin.
>
> Man has nothing that the animals have not at least a vestige of, the animals have nothing that man does not in some degree share. Since then, the animals are creatures with wants and feelings differing in degree only from our own, they surely have their rights. This fact, now beginning to be recognized by the Caucasian world, was first proclaimed by Moses and was emphasized by the Buddhists over 2,000 years ago.

Seton's books portrayed the grizzly bear as a huge but oddly fragile creature whose tragic flaw was its strength. A grizzly might kill you with a swat of its paw or crush you with a hug, but it was essentially a stoic, peaceful, misunderstood creature. Grizzlies had been persecuted down through history, but their values were our values. If you left them alone, they would return the favour. Don't crowd them, don't threaten a mother with cubs, and you'll be fine.

This was comforting advice as I lay in my sleeping bag on that dark, windy, cold night in grizzly country. But while I tried to get to sleep, I couldn't help thinking about another source of information about bears: a book called *Night of the Grizzlies.* I'd read this book earlier in the summer, and it painted a much more ominous portrait of grizzly bears. The story took place only a short distance away from where Dave and I were camped. In Glacier Park, Montana, park rangers and innkeepers had always maintained a casual and friendly relationship with bears. Guests gathered on bleachers every evening to watch the "bear show," in which grizzlies wandered down out of the forest to feed on table scraps set out for them behind the hotels. In the park's campgrounds, tourists hand-fed bear cubs and posed alongside them with their children. On the highway running through the park, there would be traffic jams when people stopped to feed the wild animals, and when a grizzly was spotted on a sidehill, amateur photographers would get involved in quiet contests of bravado to see who would get closest to the foraging bear. Again, it was supposedly against the law to feed the bears or approach them, but the bears didn't seem to mind, and let's face it, the park was in the tourism business. The resorts were trying to make a living, and the park rangers were under a certain amount of pressure to let people have their fun. What harm did it do? The official take on the bears was printed right there in the official government brochures—bears won't hurt you as long as you don't provoke them.

On the night of August 13, 1967, the bears attacked. At the campground in Trout Lake, a grizzly walked into a campsite, tore apart packs and tents, and sniffed at sleeping bags while the young campers lay frozen in terror. One of the campers punched the bear in the nose after it clawed him. The bear woofed in anger and backed away, allowing the teenagers to run for the trees and climb to safety. But a nineteen-year-old park employee named Michelle Koons couldn't open the zipper on her sleeping bag. The bear grabbed her, dragged her into the woods and began eating her alive. Perched up in the trees, her friends shouted advice but were too afraid to climb down as she begged for help. "He's ripping my arm!" she screamed. "My God, I'm dead!"

Meanwhile, ten miles away at the Granite Park Chalet, an entirely different grizzly padded into a camp and grabbed a boy named Roy Ducat in his sleeping bag. He managed to keep silent while the bear savaged him, then it moved over and attacked his nineteen-year-old girlfriend, Julie Helgeson. She screamed loudly enough to wake up campers hundreds of yards away as the bear dragged her into the woods and began eating her. The next day, the park rangers shot four grizzly bears, two of which had human blood in their claws and other physical evidence linking them to the killings of the two girls.

These incidents would have been horrifying enough if they had happened during one summer, but the fact that they occurred at the same time, only ten miles apart, with victims that were both attractive young women of the same age, generated lurid headlines around the world. There was speculation that violent thunderstorms or LSD-spiked snacks might have driven the normally docile bears into a homicidal rage, and some biologists theorized that it was the scent of menstrual blood that attracted the bears. (Both women were having their period.) How could normal, healthy bears have perpetrated these horrifying attacks? It violated every principle of what biologists understood—or thought they understood—about grizzlies. The immediate impulse was to blame the people, and for several years after the attacks, park brochures warned menstruating women that they might be risking danger of attack. But then a series of scientific field tests determined that, while polar bears were attracted to bloody tampons, grizzly bears didn't show much interest. Some thought it was all about park politics and that safety had been sacrificed for the sake of tourist dollars. Others thought the attacks were the inevitable consequence of bears losing their fear of humans. Whatever the cause, the so-called "night of the grizzlies" marked a tidal shift in the management of bears in the United States. As a result of the attacks, the Parks Service closed the dumps, killed garbage-habituated bears and installed steel strongboxes for food in back-country campsites. In brochures, visitors were warned that bears were now considered dangerous. Park rangers cautioned tourists that attacks, while rare, could occur suddenly and without provocation.

Some bear experts blended that advice with assurances that attacks and injuries were incredibly rare. They insisted that grizzlies are essentially vegetarians. One much-cited piece of reassurance was that the average citizen is "more likely to be killed by a bee than a grizzly bear." These reminders made for good biology but dubious statistical analysis, since bears will happily eat meat anytime they can get it, and the average citizen is also much more likely to encounter a bee than a grizzly bear. In any case, who cares about the odds of being eaten if you happen to be the chump who wins the lottery? So August 13, 1967, marked the end of something and the beginning of something else. It was like Altamont, the day the music died. It left people once again not knowing what to think about bears. Is the grizzly bear a misunderstood vegetarian or the four-legged equivalent of a great white shark?

Back home in the city, I hadn't worried much about these questions. Like most people, I couldn't see how they affected my life one way or another. But, camped out that cold, windy night in the heart of grizzly country, I thought about them quite a bit.

* * * *

For the next couple of weeks, Dave and I explored every back road we could find. When one road dead-ended at the ocean at Prince Rupert, British Columbia, we loaded the van onto a ferry and cruised for a day and a half through the Inside Passage, slipping through fjords and narrow inlets with killer whales and Pacific white-sided dolphins cavorting alongside the ship. Back on land, we cruised up and down remote highways and camped out along rivers at night. We carried a tin pail in the back of the van that contained the congealed remains of the previous night's stew. I had brought along some fishing gear and a little .22 rifle, and just about every evening we'd try to acquire some wild food to put in the stew pot before heating it up. It never occurred to us that we were risking ptomaine poisoning by eating the same stew night after night and never refrigerating it. We reasoned that simmering it for half an hour would kill anything harmful in the mixture. And we must have been right, because we ate it every evening and didn't seem to die.

As soon as we got our tents set up, I'd walk along the river and cast a little Mepps spinner into the fast water, hoping to catch a fish. It wasn't usually very long before a hyperactive little trout pounced on the lure. I'd wind him in, admire the multicoloured little guy, then knock him on the head with a rock and slip him in my knapsack. Sometimes while I was fishing, Dave would take the .22 and prowl the woods, looking for a grouse. One night I was walking back to the tent with the fishing rod in my hand when a car pulled up and an unsavoury-looking guy rolled down the window and started asking questions—How was the fishing? Where did I live? and so on. He got out of the car, reached into his jacket, pulled out a Bowie knife and asked, "Did you ever see a knife this big?" I was starting to get a little apprehensive, when Dave walked out of the bush. We talked for a while, with Dave standing off to one side with the rifle resting in the crook of his arm; then the guy left, leaving us wondering whether he was a harmless oddball or a lunatic.

Most evenings, as we explored the surrounding area, I scrutinized the animal tracks printed in the sand and mud of the riverbank. It was a boyhood habit, picked up from reading adventure books about the outdoors, and I was obsessive enough about it that I could tell the difference between the fore and hind footprints of a coyote, a heron track from a raven, and a mink track from a squirrel. I saw lots of black bear tracks—no big deal; I'd seen plenty of black bears. But no grizzly tracks. There's considerable variation in size, but you can tell the two species apart by subtle differences in the toes and claws. With its long hind foot, heel pad and five toes, a grizzly track looks very much like the print made by a flat-footed human, albeit one with exceedingly long claws. (One early historian described a large grizzly track as resembling the "footprint of a Negro.") I wanted to see fresh grizzly tracks and not to see them, since seeing them meant I would have to hasten back to the tent and suggest to Dave that we should probably find a different campsite.

My ambition to see a grizzly was by no means the reason for the trip, but the more I didn't see a grizzly, the more I wanted to see one. I had a sense that if you saw a grizzly, you might have a slightly better understanding of nature, which in turn might give you a microscopically better understanding of the world. So I kept my eyes peeled as we camped out along the Skeena River, the Kispiox and the upper Fraser. There were no grizzlies in sight, but there *were* lots of good grizzly stories if you sought them out. In a log-panelled restaurant in Williams Lake, we struck up a conversation with a provincial conservation officer. After we'd quizzed him for a while about grizzlies, the officer leaned forward and parted his hair to show us a scar on the side of his head. A grizzly had almost cost him his life, he said. The incident had taken place a couple of years before, near Fort St. John, British Columbia, in the traditional country of the Dunneza people, who are more commonly known as the Beaver Indians. A Dunneza trapper named Harvey Cardinal had heard about a large grizzly that, for some reason, was roaming around the forest in the middle of January. The Beavers have lived with grizzlies for many centuries and believe that the best way to coexist with the bears is to stay clear of them. But Cardinal was a sturdy, fearless man who had spent most of his life in the bush and wasn't afraid of grizzlies. He also knew the bear's rich winter pelt would be worth a lot of money. So he loaded his rifle and set out to track down the bear.

Most animals, both predator and prey, tend to double back on their trail in a buttonhook pattern before bedding down. In this way they can use their nose to monitor the upwind quadrant and their eyes to guard against trouble coming from downwind. There's no peace of mind for any animal; even a large bear must remain forever vigilant against the possibility of an even bigger bear showing up. So the grizzly hooked back and bedded down in thick cover, just a few yards upwind of its own trail. It was thirty below zero. It was so cold Harvey was wearing mitts. He should have been wearing gloves. He was carrying an old Lee-Enfield .303 rifle, and it would have been a lot easier to switch off the safety catch and fire a shot with gloves.

As he followed the bear's big shuffling tracks in the snow, he unknowingly walked past the clump of undergrowth in which the bear was bedded. The bear allowed him to walk by, then sprang after him and shattered his skull with a single blow. When his friends came looking for Harvey the next day, they found him lying on his back, frozen stiff. His mitts were still on his hands, he hadn't touched the safety, and his upper body was cleaned off down to the backbone.

Our conservation officer told us he had attended the scene and decided this was a dangerous bear. If it had killed one man and eaten him, it might learn from that experience and decide to do it again. He rounded up a helicopter and a pilot and went searching for the bear. It was cold, painstaking work inside the cramped cockpit, flying just above the treetops hour after hour and peering down through the trees to see the bear's tracks before the rotors blew them in. Finally, towards the end of the day, they flushed the grizzly from an evergreen thicket and the conservation officer opened the door and shot it several times from the air. The pilot set the machine down next to the bear's body and the officer climbed out. There are many stories of the grizzly's ability to soak up multiple gunshots, so the officer was nervous as he exited the chopper with his gun aimed at the theoretically dead man-eater. Concentrating on the bear, taking a few steps sideways, he walked into the still-turning tail rotor. "It struck me a glancing blow and sliced off a piece of my skull," he said, showing us where the surgeons had installed a plate over his brain. "Lucky for me, the tail rotor wasn't damaged, so they were able to fly me out unconscious, or I would have died on the spot."

He said the bear turned out to be an old but healthy male, five hundred pounds in weight, with the remains of Harvey Cardinal in its stomach. The wildlife biologists had no explanation for why it was on the move in January instead of sleeping in its den, but the conservation officer said that that alone was a valuable lesson in grizzly bear behaviour. "It shouldn't have killed Harvey and ate him," he said. "But it shouldn't have been out roaming around in deep snow in the middle of winter either."

He said that if we were looking for grizzly bears, we might try the Bella Coola Valley, a couple of hundred miles west of Williams Lake. He said grizzlies gathered there in the late summer and early fall for the salmon migration. "But there's no guarantee that you'll actually see one," he said. "You could spend your whole life in this country and never see a grizzly. Or you could run into one in the parking lot behind this restaurant. They're very unpredictable. Every time you think you know something about grizzlies, some bear will do something that makes you realize you don't know them at all."

* * * *

So we headed for Bella Coola. And as we drove west across the high plateau, I thought about friends of mine who had seen grizzlies without really trying. My friend Susan had gone on a canoe trip on the Teslin River in the Yukon Territory with her girlfriends. Some of them had read *Night of the Grizzlies* and decided they wouldn't camp anywhere they saw fresh tracks. By the end of the first day they realized they wouldn't be able to camp at all if they kept this rule, so they pitched their tents on the trampled sandbars and lay wide-eyed in their tents at night, listening to salmon splashing in the river and wondering when a bear was going to show up.

One night they heard a large animal splashing in the river, then dead silence, then a frightful clattering as the creature charged up the stony beach towards their tents. They screamed in unison as the animal hit the guy rope and brought the tent down. Climbing frantically out of the collapsed tent, they got their flashlights out and looked around. The big animal was gone, but they saw from the tracks in the sand that it had been only a moose. The next day they paddled around a corner in their canoes and a massive grizzly was standing in the river, right in their path. They stopped paddling and froze, as the current carried them right towards the bear. It stood up and watched them, water dripping from its fur as they glided past just thirty feet away.

My friend Paul had seen a grizzly too and had told me about it earlier that summer in a postcard he sent me from Great Bear Lake. He was working as a fishing guide up there, and was boating across the lake with his guests one day when they saw a sow grizzly bear swimming from one island to another with her two cubs. He drove towards the bears and pulled up alongside to have a good look at them as they dog-paddled along, rolling their eyes in consternation as the boat approached. Mother grizzlies have an automatic response to the appearance of any predator: anger. When Paul drew up alongside, the sow grizzly immediately recognized him and his tourists as ancient foes. And when she got to shore, she did a sort of murderous dance on the tundra, rocking back and forth on stiffened legs, popping her jaws, slapping the ground and tearing great mouthfuls from the sod—all of which was meant to demonstrate what she would do if they followed her any farther.

I wasn't exactly a seasoned traveller, but I had noticed that everything turns out to be a little different than you expect.

Whether you crash a car into a tree, lose your way in the wilderness or meet the mayor of your city in the checkout line at the liquor store there is inevitably some offbeat element of the experience. I didn't want to rely on stories about grizzly bears. I wanted to see one for myself, and I knew that if Dave and I spent enough time knocking around the desolate back roads of British Columbia, we'd eventually see one.

So our quest continued. The first half of the road trip from Williams Lake and Bella Coola turned out to be wide-open range country, with lots of rolling grassland and dry-country pine. Some people call this part of British Columbia the Cariboo country, or the Chilcotin Plateau. We stopped in dusty little communities like Riske Creek, Kleena Kleene, and Alexis Creek, where horses were tied up in front of the post office and old-timers hobbled around in beat-up cowboy boots and sweat-stained Stetson hats. This is real cowboy country, and has been for a long time. Near Alexis Creek we saw a monument to a rancher named Norman Lee, who in 1898 decided to drive two hundred cattle from here to the Yukon Territory, where he planned to sell the beef for a big profit to Klondike gold mining camps. It was a fifteen-hundred-mile walk, and the cattle began to starve, so he killed them, loaded the meat onto scows and tried to barge them across Teslin Lake. But the barges swamped in an October storm and he threw in the towel and went home, leaving all those neatly butchered sides of beef bobbing in the freezing waves. The Chilcotin Plateau ends at a town called Anahim Lake, where it T-bones against a wall of rock a mile high. At the gas station in Anahim Lake, the attendant looked at our dust-caked van and said, "Where you headed?"

"Bella Coola."

"You won't make it in that little thing. Most of the folks around here only travel the road when they have to, and they use a four-wheel-drive truck with a winch on the front."

We went for a beer at the local saloon. Anahim Lake seemed to be the sort of place where grizzlies weren't welcome, judging by all the skulls nailed to the wall. A cowboy nodded out the window at our GMC van. "I hope you're not going to Bella Coola in that little piece of crap."

He told us the road was forbidding. Not very long ago, it was nothing more than a treacherous mountain footpath used by the Indians. Before the white man arrived, the Indians subsisted on something called "grease," a foul-smelling paste made from eulachon fish. He said the wealthier Indians, like the Chilcotins and the Nuxalks, didn't want to break their backs carrying the grease across the mountains, so they left the job to a tribe called the Carriers. For many centuries the Carriers packed the grease over the coastal mountains, and that hair-raising footpath became known as the Grease Trail. In 1793 along came Alexander Mackenzie, looking for a route to the Pacific Ocean. He was planning to canoe down the Fraser River to the ocean, where the city of Vancouver now sits, but inland natives told him the Indians down there were hostile to visitors and would probably kill him. So he took the Grease Trail instead. When he reached salt water, the Nuxalk Indians, who lived in Bella Coola, weren't very happy to see him either. But they let him paint a few words on a rock before running him off ("Alexander Mackenzie, from Canada, by land, the twenty-second of July, one thousand, seven hundred and ninety-three"). "Everybody thinks Lewis and Clark made history when they crossed the continent in 1805," said the cowboy. "But Alexander Mackenzie did it first."

Throughout the 1930s and 1940s, the folks who lived in Bella Coola pestered the government to build a road over the mountain range along the old Grease Trail. The provincial road engineers examined the route and said it was impossible. So in the early 1950s a handful of can-do pioneering types from Bella Coola and Anahim Lake decided they would show the government how to get her done. With a couple of bulldozers and plenty of dynamite and volunteer muscle, they started at opposite ends and worked towards the middle, cutting switchbacks up one side of those mountains and down the other. In some places, the road was little more than a narrow ledge hacked along the side of a cliff. In other places, the grades were so steep that, going up, they'd have to hook a cable to a big tree and inch their trucks up the hill on the winch. Descending the other side, they'd have to stop at little pull-offs to let their brakes cool. In September 1953 the two bulldozers ploughed aside the last trees and boulders and kissed blades. With characteristic aplomb, the locals dubbed the white-knuckle route over the summit "The Hill."

After overnighting in a campground at Anahim Lake, Dave and I pushed on towards Bella Coola, heading west through thickening forest and gradually climbing The Hill. The road was rough gravel and crushed rock. In some places, the hairpin at the top of the switchback was so abrupt that it seemed impossible to make the turn, and we debated whether it would be easier just to dispense with the turnaround and continue up the next switchback in reverse. As we climbed the mountain, the valley fell away beneath us, a misty chasm that seemed all the more fearsome because there was no guardrail or shoulder. All we needed was a blown tire or overheated brake shoe and we'd be over the edge. We played Roy Acuff and the Smoky Mountain

Boys to impart a sporting air to the enterprise, but when we got far enough up the mountain it became clear that we were past the point of no return, and we began to wonder if we should have listened to the warning from the old guy in the saloon. In Darwinian terms, we were doing what young animals do. We had left the custody of our mothers, and now we were exploring the edges of our territory. If we died, it would prove our stupidity and would therefore be of no great loss to the gene pool.

On some of the steep grades, the mountain was exposed to the mood swings of the weather and the road was eroded with deep gouges. On one switchback, Dave had to climb ahead of the vehicle, filling in the ruts by dropping large chunks of rock into the holes and smoothing them over with crushed rock that he swept and stamped with his feet. While he worked, I sat in the van with my foot jammed on the brake and the front bumper pointed towards the sky. My little Handi-Van had a standard transmission, and getting it moving forward again required keeping the left foot on the clutch and the right foot on the brake. Without reducing the pressure on the brake, I had to depress the accelerator with my right foot, then rev the engine to a high, chattering whine while simultaneously easing off the clutch. As soon as the clutch bit, the little van would start to slide backwards, slewing madly, spitting rocks; then, pausing and roaring, it would begin to stubbornly claw its way skyward. Dave would stand a little ways up the grade, cheering and shouting encouragement, but I couldn't help noticing that he didn't bother to ride along. I wouldn't have ridden along either if there had been a choice. It was a clear free-fall off the crumbled shoulder of the road, and I kept the driver's door cracked open as the van whined and wheel-hopped up the hill.

By late afternoon we were over the summit and rolling down into the Bella Coola Valley. One of the sweet rewards of travelling across the country by land rather than air is crossing the coastal divide and experiencing the moment of sudden climate change that happens when you cross a mountain range. In the course of a few thousand feet, we descended from the bare rock and snow of the summit to the greenery of the alpine zone to the enlarging trees of the temperate forest to the ferns and lush rainforest of the Bella Coola Valley.

Flanked on both sides by snow-capped mountains, the valley looks like one of those sun-drenched, luminous western landscapes painted by Bierstadt or one of the other German romantics. Towering above us was a rocky citadel that Alexander Mackenzie had described in his journal as "a mountain of stupendous proportion." On the back side of Mount Stupendous was a dark cloud trailing misty veils of rain, or perhaps snow. The sun lanced through the cloud and created a rainbow over the glistening black rock and crisp white snow of the summit. Farther along the horizon were Mount Defiance and Thunder Mountain. It was a display of tectonic geology so magnificent you couldn't do much more than look at it for three or four minutes and then shrug and carry on.

The Hill deterred most drivers, so we didn't see any Winnebagos, campgrounds or the rest of the trashy sprawl that characterizes most of scenic North America. Once we came down off the mountain, the highway looped through heavy forest and open meadow. Picturesque ranch houses and old barns sat along the foot of mountain walls, and the traffic was so light that when we stopped to take a photograph on the bridge above the Bella Coola River, we loitered there at mid-bridge for at least fifteen minutes without a single vehicle going by. We needed to find a place to camp for the night. But first, as a matter of principle, we wanted to drive down to salt water, so we carried on for another twenty miles or so to the village of Bella Coola, where we parked by the government pier and walked out to the end of the dock. Ever since I saw the words "Bella Coola" printed on the edge of the continent on an old Rand McNally globe in our Grade 6 classroom, I had wanted to visit this little community, and now here I was.

We hadn't seen any grizzlies, but we had seen many good road signs. We had visited Kleena Kleene, Riske Creek, Likely, Spuzzum, Horsefly, Ta Ta Creek and now Bella Coola. The mountains were arrayed above the ocean in an operatic manner that seemed to say "Aim Camera Here," but as always, reaching the edge of the continent was a bit of an anticlimax. The ocean was chalky green and smelled of dead fish. A number of beat-up commercial fishing boats were tied up in the harbour, but other than a few forlorn gulls sitting on the bridge timbers, there wasn't a sign of life.

After we had finished paying homage to the Pacific, we went looking for a place to camp for the night. Bella Coola is mostly a reserve for the Nuxalk Indians—a smallish community of government homes with derelict cars and half-repaired fishing boats sitting up on blocks in the yards. It looked rundown, but the kids doodling around on their banana bikes appeared to be sleek and happy, and as we cruised the back roads of the village, everyone waved. We'd pass pedestrians, they'd wave and we'd wave back. Sometimes we forgot to wave and immediately felt like rude city people. We saw very little in the way of majestic grizzlies standing by the edge of the sea scooping out salmon with their forepaws. With spectacular nature footage, television and movies have permanently warped the public's understanding of the world. Thanks to an endless diet of wildlife erotica, we tend to associate all the world's ecosystems with the glamorous predators that supposedly thrive there. The first time I visited Long Island, I was hesitant to go in the ocean because I suspected ominous music would start playing and the dorsal fin of a great white shark would pop from the surf. When city people visit the wilderness, they think wolves and bears are lurking behind every tree. But you can spend your entire life in ideal habitat and never once encounter a big predator. Just ask people from Colorado if they've ever run into a mountain lion, or the exchange student from Senegal if he's ever seen a leopard. Large predators occupy the top of the food chain, so they are few and far between, and getting an appointment with one isn't easy. There aren't too many grizzlies at the best of times, and they avoid people, so I was beginning to accept that, just as the game warden had cautioned us, it was possible to spend your whole life in prime grizzly bear country and never see one.

As we drove through the village, we pulled up to an old-timer who was standing on the side of the road, chatted with him for a few minutes and asked him if there were many bears around. He laughed and said, "Try the dump"—which, of course, for bear watchers is the last refuge of a scoundrel. We drove to the dump, where a dozen or so black bears waddled around in the garbage. Some were so wide-assed and corpulent that merely walking a few steps on level ground caused them to pant in bleary-eyed exhaustion. Is there any animal in the world more debauched than a black bear in a garbage dump? One of them waded through a heap of burning trash and sat wearily on a heap of burning pallets. The fact that his fur and broad rump were on fire seemed to register only gradually on his dim brain. There were no grizzlies in sight, and even if there were, a bear in a dump is not a real bear, so we kept rolling.

As we headed back up-valley, we stopped to pick up a guy who was hitch-hiking with his little dog. He was a woolly-haired transient with muddy pants and a beard halfway down his chest. "Where are you going?" I asked him.

"Mexico."

"Where are you coming from?" Dave asked.

"Alaska."

"How are you getting to Mexico?"

"I'm walking."

"Pardon?"

"I said I'm walking, down through the mountains."

Now you're talking. After many long days cooped up together in this little truck, Dave and I were ready for some foreign company, and this guy was the most interesting person we'd met so far. He told us he'd driven the route from Mexico to Alaska earlier in the year and had left caches of dried food, fresh gear and granola along the route. He and his dog, a perky terrier named Happy Dog, were following the autumn south, walking a hundred miles a week. With any luck they'd be in the Sierra Madres in three months. We guessed that he was getting sick of eating granola and invited him to join us for some of our Eternal Stew. Twenty minutes later we pulled off onto a promising-looking forest road, bumped slowly along it for several hundred yards and pulled to a stop at a small clearing overlooking the river. We set up our tents, unfurled our sleeping bags, put the stew on a low boil and prepared to do a little exploring. After many days on the road I had a routine—string up the fishing rod, strap on the filleting knife, tuck a box of small spinning lures into the shirt pocket and walk down the river, looking for a seam in the current or a boil where a little trout might be holding. If I got a trout or two, I'd clean them up and add them to the stew.

Part of the routine involved absent-mindedly scanning the sandbar as I walked along, looking for grizzly tracks. There never were any grizzly tracks, so I'd gotten casual about it. This time, however, I had walked only a few hundred yards down the riverbank when I saw something that made my heart stop: a big bear track. It was as wide as my hat, and the long claw marks were deeply impressed in the sand. Standing there, looking at the grizzly track, I spotted a second string—also grizzly tracks, but smaller, paralleling the river not thirty steps away.

As I stood there looking in amazement at the tracks, I heard a shout from the other guys. I assumed they had seen a track too, but they were pointing at the water. I walked over to join them. It was late in the afternoon and the water was so dark that I hadn't noticed that the river was alive with salmon. A deep channel ran past the end of the gravel bar, and once my eyes had adjusted, I saw what they were pointing at: dozens of big fish, their tails twisting as they shifted back and forth in the gloom. As we stood there, one of them suddenly broke from the group and powered towards the surface, jumped clear and fell back into the river.

We studied the river, and it soon became apparent that every riffle and pool was stuffed with salmon. They were rolling on the surface and splashing in the shallows. I told the others about the bear tracks and we walked back to look. They examined a track and agreed it had been made by a grizzly. Then Happy Dog found a salmon that had been bitten in half. It was lying in shallow water, its entrails and eggs torn out. But, remarkably, it was still alive, its gills moving faintly as the water pushed against it. The bear that had bitten this fish in half probably wasn't too far away, judging by the fact that the fish was still alive, so we broke off the forensic examination and walked back to the camp. I was glad we had set up our tents close together, and I noticed that, without discussing it, we had collected an extra-large stack of dry wood for the evening campfire.

Darkness fell quickly and early, as it always does in the rainforest, and we sat by the fire listening to the hiker tell stories of his long walk down the spine of the continent. He said he'd seen lots of grizzlies along the way. Earlier in the summer, he'd sometimes camped out in alpine meadows with grizzlies in clear sight only a few hundred yards away. They'd be digging for ground squirrels, setting tons of earth flying as they madly excavated the mountain. He said he saw old males, sows with cubs, young juveniles, you name it. He said the grizzlies were aware of his presence but pretty much ignored him. "I was never afraid," he said. "I could tell by their body language they weren't looking for trouble."

He was the only person I'd ever met who had actually spent a fair amount of time in close contact with grizzly bears. And he said they didn't frighten him. He said the Indians believe that bears and men are brothers, and some old hunters refuse to skin a bear because the flayed carcass looks like the torso of a man. He said that whenever he met a grizzly, he raised his arm in greeting, to let the bear know he came as a brother. He said living with bears and other creatures in the wilderness for long periods of time had taught him to sympathize with the grizzly bear's point of view. He said he didn't like to admit it, but he was developing a fear of the human race. Pickup trucks with men in them made him nervous. Walking south through the mountains, he sooner or later had to cross roads, and had gotten into the habit of waiting in the brush alongside the highway until the cars were gone before loping across. He said he had come down off the mountain trail to have a look at Bella Coola because he thought it had a pretty name.

Every fifteen minutes or so, as we talked and told stories and poked at the fire with our sticks, Happy Dog leapt up from his resting place at his master's feet and started barking, running forward to the outer edge of the campfire light and yapping furiously at something only he could hear. Whenever this happened, I paused, looking out into the impenetrable blackness, wondering if I was going to hear the crunching footsteps of an approaching grizzly. I don't know what our guest thought because he didn't express an opinion, other than patiently reassuring his dog. Once in a while we heard a violent splash in the river. But the salmon jumped so regularly that it was hard to tell whether we were just hearing the ordinary thrashing of a salmon or the splashing of a bear.

All night long the dog barked at regular intervals, and I slept so little that it was a relief when daylight finally seeped through the wet fabric of the tent. Our plan was to drop our guest and Happy Dog on the flank of The Hill, where they would continue their hike to Mexico. Then Dave and I would begin wending our way back home. It was almost the end of August, and the cottonwoods along the river were turning yellow. University would be starting up again in about ten days, and we had eighteen hundred miles of driving ahead of us. But first we needed to go down to take one last look at the river.

It wasn't quite raining, but particles of mist were drifting in the air. Raindrops are supposed to fall, but these water droplets floated as weightlessly as pollen. The entire valley of the river was thick with the smell of cedar and decomposing fish. Salmon finned belly-up in the shallows. With their hooked bills and empty eye sockets, they drifted like sarcophagi. When the baby salmon hatched, they would feed on the crumpled bodies of their parents, their only chance of surviving in this infertile mountain river. The salmon were dying so their offspring could live, and the entire river valley was heavy with the incessant splashing and musty smell of this ancient tragedy. I couldn't find any new bear tracks on the shore, so it was obvious that no grizzlies had crossed the sandbar during the night. Maybe they had avoided the area once we set up camp and built a fire. But why was Happy Dog barking all night? Perhaps a bear had crept through the woods and studied us from beyond the firelight.

I placed my foot beside the grizzly track. I had to admit that the main feeling I had experienced from camping in these woods was a low-level nervousness that now and then quickened into fear. But I didn't want to discount that feeling. I knew that fear is not to be underestimated as an educational tool. As Dr. Johnson pointed out, nothing concentrates the mind like the prospect of one's imminent hanging. This felt like a place where lessons could be learned. Measuring my foot against the footprint of the bear, I made a little resolution to come back here one day and get a good look at the animal that made this track.

The Horrible Bear

Many years passed before I returned to Bella Coola, during which I did some occasional reading on the subject of the grizzly bear and began to understand that the "grizzly bear," which is scientifically classified as *Ursus horribilus,* is just a North American version of *Ursus arctos,* the "brown bear," a diversified species that shows up in different models all around the world. When I went to the Moscow Circus as a kid, those clownish Russian bears that rode around on bicycles were essentially grizzly bears. The bears that live in the mountains of Italy and France are also essentially grizzlies, and so was the old bear in short pants that I once saw dancing to a gypsy concertina on a street corner in Macedonia. Genetically, they are all the same animal.

During the last ice age, about fifty thousand years ago, so much water was locked up in glacial ice that the level of the oceans was lower than it is now. North America and Siberia were connected by a land bridge, and all kinds of animals were able to migrate back and forth. By carbon-dating ancient bones, scientists are able to track the migration of brown bears and other animals as they moved from Siberia and into what is now Alaska and Canada. But the brown bears didn't have an easy time of it. They faced two great obstacles: a wall of glacial ice that separated Alaska from the rest of the continent, and a mega-predator called the short-faced bear.

The short-faced bear (*Arctodus simus*) was the largest bear that ever lived, and during the Pleistocene it was the largest predator on earth. About twice the size of a big male grizzly, it stood about six feet high at the shoulder and weighed about a ton. With its long legs and extremely efficient cardiovascular system, it was able to run down almost any animal it could see. It had a nose that was twice as large and effective as the grizzly's, and it could smell food six miles away. Unlike other bears, which are omnivorous, the short-faced bear was carnivorous. It hunted animals like elk, sloths and camels. When the opportunity came along, it robbed the kills of other predators like dire wolves, sabre-toothed cats and grizzlies. No predator of the time would have stood its ground before an approaching short-faced bear.

For some reason, the giant bison, camels, mastodons and other mega-fauna that inhabited North America died off about twelve thousand years ago. Scientists aren't in agreement about why this happened. Some believe that the climate warmed up faster than the animals' ability to adapt. There is also a theory that there was a cataclysmic die-off, based on evidence that a meteor exploded in the atmosphere almost thirteen thousand years ago and created a sort of nuclear winter that wiped out most of the species that were around at the time (as happened with the dinosaurs millions of years ago). Another theory is that human hunters exterminated most of the big herbivores, or at least pressured them to the point where their populations could no longer recover. This theory might seem dubious, but the aboriginal population was then about ten times what it is now. (Demographers have estimated the ancient population at about ten million). And the big mammals began disappearing a few centuries after the development of the Clovis point, a sharp and deadly weapon that first appeared in North America about thirteen thousand years ago. Propelled with an ivory *atlatl,* or throwing stick, the Clovis-tipped spear was the Stone Age equivalent of the high-powered rifle. Armed with this technology, bands of roving hunters could encircle and kill any large, ponderous plant-eaters they encountered. Accompanied by dogs, which at that time were essentially domesticated wolves, the hunters could even harass and kill large, dangerous animals like mastodons and bears.

Clovis points are still valuable—a good one with a certificate of authenticity will fetch a thousand dollars—but their value has more to do with their hand-crafted beauty than their scarcity. They were in use from northern Canada to the Gulf of Mexico, and it's not inconceivable that Clovis-equipped hunters might have pushed some species to extinction. And when the mega-herbivores disappeared, mega-predators like the sabre-toothed cats and short-faced bears died off along with them. Once the short-faced bears were out of the way, grizzlies migrated south and proliferated throughout North America. They particularly thrived on the open country, where grasses, berry bushes and ungulate animals like caribou, bison and elk provided an abundant food supply.

When the first European explorers came to North America four centuries ago, they found a continent that was overrun by bears. The home range of grizzly bears spread from the Arctic down through the prairies and all the way west to the Pacific and down through the mountains into what is now Mexico. The abundance of plant life and animals on the prairies meant there were grizzlies everywhere. In 1691 the Hudson's Bay Company sent an Englishman named Henry Kelsey on a thousand-mile journey from Fort York on Hudson Bay to the plains of western Saskatchewan. In his journal, Kelsey wrote that he and his Assiniboine guide reached the prairies on the evening of August 20. As far as they could see there was "nothing but short round sticky grass and buffalo and a great sort of a bear which is bigger than any white bear and is neither white nor black but silver hair'd like our English rabbit." Later Kelsey and his native guide encountered two large brown bears at close range. The bears charged, chasing the Assiniboine up a tree and Kelsey into a thick clump of woods, from where he shot and killed both bears with his flintlock musket, winning for himself the footnote of being the first white man in North America to bag one of the bears. Because of their imposing size and frightening behaviour, Kelsey described them as "grisly bears" in his journal.

In 1805, when Lewis and Clark crossed the Great Plains, the Indians warned them about those prairie grizzlies (which Meriwether Lewis called "white bears" because of their grizzled fur.) In his journal entry for April 13, 1805, Lewis observed, "When the Indians are about to go in quest of the white bear, previous to their departure, they paint themselves and perform all those supersticious rights commonly observed when they are about to make war uppon a neighbouring nation."

Being a typical explorer, Lewis was generally dismissive of the natives, and didn't attach much credibility to their warnings about grizzlies. His party carried rifles, not bows and arrows, and he couldn't imagine any animal standing up to a hail of well-aimed musket balls from his hunters. But a couple of weeks later, Lewis met a bear face to face, and the experience turned out to be a little more harrowing than he expected. He and a couple of his hunters were out looking for game when they encountered a pair of grizzlies. They shot one of the bears, but it ran away as if the bullets had had no effect. The other bear charged, and they just managed to gun it down it before it reached them. Rather than being white, as Lewis expected, the bears were yellowish brown. "The legs of this bear are somewhat longer than those of the black, as are its tallons and tusks . . . the eyes small black and piercing."

A few days later they ran into another bear, and this one was just as difficult to dispatch. "In the evening we saw a Brown or Grisley beare on a sand beech, I went out with one man Geo Drewyer & Killed the bear, which was verry large and a turrible looking animal, which we found verry hard to kill we Shot ten Balls into him before we killed him, & 5 of those Balls through his lights This animal is the largest of the carnivorous kind I ever saw we had nothing that could way him, I think his weight may be stated at 500 pounds [227 kilograms]. . . . we had him skined and divided, the oile tried up & put in Kegs for use."

This happened again and again. The great bears seemed to be everywhere, and would often charge on sight. "These bear being so hard to die reather intimidates us all," he wrote. "I must confess that I do not like the gentlemen and had reather fight two Indians than one bear." By the end of the expedition, he and his men were sleeping with their guns at their sides, and Lewis believed that only the "hand of Providence" had saved them from losing someone to a grizzly bear.

Not all the early explorers agreed that the grizzly was a troublemaker. Zebulon Pike, who explored the southwest in 1807, suggested that the bears were essentially peaceful animals that displayed the admirable personality characteristics of America itself. He argued that adult bears seldom attack unless provoked, and when they do, they "defend themselves courageously." Pike returned to Washington and gave two well-behaved captive grizzly bears to President Thomas Jefferson, who kept them in pens on the White House lawn. But in the view of most nineteenth-century ranchers and settlers, the grizzly was a dangerous beast, a modern-day Grendel that needed to be vanquished before the land could truly be made safe for human commerce. The Pennsylvania naturalist John Godman summed up a common opinion when he described the grizzly bear as a "despotic and sanguinary monarch of the wilds . . . terrific in aspect . . . [and] ferociously bloodthirsty."

Around the same time as the fur traders of the Hudson's Bay Company were penetrating the continent from the north, Meriwether Lewis and other explorers were coming from the east, and Spanish explorers were working their way northward into what is now California. The grizzlies were getting boxed in from all sides, but they didn't know it yet. Exploring up through California, the Spaniards found a country that was crawling with what they called "grizzled" bears. For the same reasons that California later became a paradise for human beings, it was an Eden for grizzly bears—the mild climate allowed the animals to forgo hibernation and feed year round on the abundant berries, acorns, nuts, succulent roots, plums and wild grapes that grew on the hillsides of the Santa Ana mountains, the San Gabriels and the other coastal ranges. The rivers teemed with annual runs of salmon, and the Pacific shore was an open-air buffet of molluscs, fish and seafood. A washed-up whale might attract dozens of bears. And because food was so abundant, the animals dispensed with the usual territorial aggression that character-izes their behaviour and fed peacefully side by side, in much the same way that large groups of grizzlies will strike a temporary pact to feed communally on salmon in northern rivers.

The Spaniards, with their infatuation with blood and sacri-fice, were intrigued by the ferocity of the bears and went out of their way to engage the animals in *mano a mano* combat. A swords-man of some repute named Ramon Carrillo once overtook a huge grizzly in the Encino Valley, challenged him and fought him single-handed with a light sword. Carrillo was travelling from Santa Barbara to Los Angeles with a party of military men when they sighted the bear on the San Fernando plain. They surrounded the old grizzly, which promptly stood up like a man and offered defi-ance. "Stand back, please, *senores,*" requested Carrillo, dismount-ing and drawing his sword. "Allow me to fight a personal duel with this grand old gladiator."

His fellow travellers formed a wide circle and leaned forward in their saddles to watch the contest. According to one account of the fight, Ramon

> advanced like a dancing master, flourishing the rapier-like blade which he always carried. Bruin stood on the defensive, staring with angry astonishment. Deftly and with a smile and a banter always on his lips the young

Californian, with all the skill and grace of a trained bullfighter, danced around the grizzled giant and got in his stinging, maddening thrusts here and there. The grizzly rushed him time and again with terrific roars, but the man waited only long enough to sting the huge menacing paws with the rapier point and then side-stepped to safety. The excitement of the picturesque mounted audience grew almost beyond control, and the "vivas!" first for the caballero and then for the bear, drove the animal duelist almost frantic. With utmost coolness and always laughing Ramon Carrillo fenced with that grizzly for one hour. When all concerned seemed to be tiring of the sport he stepped in and with a quick thrust to the heart laid the splendid brute low.

In 1769 a Spanish explorer named Gaspar de Portola scouted the country near the modern California town of Morro Bay and encountered large numbers of grizzly bears. One of his mates, Miguel Costanso, recorded in his journal that they found "troops" of grizzlies in a canyon near the modern-day community of Los Osos, which in Spanish means "the bears." Costanso writes that the grizzlies

had the land plowed up and full of holes which they make in searching for the roots they live on, which the land produces. The natives also use these roots for food, and there are some of a good relish and taste. Some of the soldiers, attracted by the chase because they had been successful on two other occasions, mounted their horses and this time succeeded in shooting one.

They however experienced the fierceness and anger of these animals—when they feel themselves to be wounded, headlong they charge the hunter, who can only escape by the swiftness of his horse, for the first burst of speed is more rapid than one might expect from the bulk and awkwardness of such brutes.

The Spanish soon discovered that a couple of skilled *vaqueros* mounted on horses and armed with nothing more than rawhide lariats could dominate almost any bear they encountered. They would harass it into the open and then bait the frustrated animal until they were able to lasso its legs and neck from opposite directions. The bears learned about horses and ropes, and on some occasions a large, older animal would simply sit down and, with dexterous paws, reel in the horse and rider. But the horses were smart and bred for this work, and they had their own tricks, using sudden bursts of speed and changes of direction to jerk the bear off its feet. Restrained by a web of ropes, the bears could be led into town as an entertainment for their captors' friends and family. Once the bears were shown off, they would be penned up in preparation for one of the most popular diversions in early California: a bull and bear fight.

In the mid-1800s the high point of any Sunday afternoon in California was a fight to the death between the two animals. The contests were promoted with all the fanfare and razzmatazz of today's heavyweight boxing matches—in a carnival atmosphere that celebrated an imminent showdown between the two seasoned pugilists. Some bears became scarred gladiators with many victories against large fighting bulls. According to the promoters, the animals were itching to get at each other, but in fact the biggest problem was getting them to fight. Prior to the match, the bear would be deprived of food and water for three or four days to make it desperate, while the bull would be tormented with sharp sticks to arouse its fury.

In one typical battle, in September 1857, placards and posters erected all over the little mining community of Mokelumme Hill, California, advertised that "WAR! WAR! WAR!" was brewing between two large fighting bulls and a bear advertised as "The Celebrated Bull-Killing Bear General Scott." A journalist named John Borthwick attended the contest and reported that General Scott, "a pretty large bear of about twelve hundred pounds," was hauled into the ring and dumped from his cage, only to scamper back into the cage as it was being pulled out of the ring. With considerable difficulty, the bear was driven once again from its cage into the arena, where it promptly dug a shallow pit in one end and tried to lie flat so as not to be conspicuous. The first bull was prodded from its enclosure with sharpened sticks. Then bars were dropped over the entrance to its pen as soon as the bull exited. But the bull no sooner saw the grizzly than it smashed through the bars and ran back into its pen, only to re-encounter an onslaught of prodding sticks. Finally the bull ran out into the arena and charged the bear. The animals grappled and the bear seized the bull's nose and threw it down. Badly torn by the bear's teeth and claws, the bull retreated to the corner and wouldn't fight. At this point, the promoters released the second bull. Both bulls charged the bear, and according to Borthwick, "the poor General between the two did not know what to do, but struck blindly with his fore-paws with such a suppliant pitiable look that I thought this the most disgusting part of the whole exhibition."

These bull and bear fights were not just popular in the rough mining camps of the backwoods. They took place in the cities too, where gentlemen of affluent means, mothers with babies in their arms and children of all ages could be found in the audience. In November 1855, a gent named Hinton Helper was relaxing in his hotel room in downtown San Francisco when he heard the sound of a parade coming. Fife and drum and clarinet music brought him to the window, where he saw a crowd of celebrants accompanying "a tremendous grizzly bear, caged, and drawn by four spirited horses." Affixed to the cage was a large poster: "FUN BREWING—HARD FIGHTING TO BE DONE ! TWO BULLS AND ONE BEAR!" The fight was held in an improvised arena in front of a mission church at four o'clock in the afternoon. Mr. Helper went to the arena box office, paid his three dollars and went inside to take a seat among the several thousand San Franciscans who had gathered for the spectacle.

The animals were brought into the arena and goaded into fighting, and Mr. Helper reported that it was

> a stirring sight to see these infuriated and muscular antagonists struggling to take each other's life. . . . Finally however, fatigued, exhausted, writhing with pain and weltering in sweat and gore, they waived the quarrel and separated, as if by mutual consent. Neither was subdued, yet both felt a desire to suspend, for a time at least, all further hostilities. The bull, now exhausted and panting, cast a pacific eye towards the bear, and seemed to sue for an armistice; the bear, bleeding and languid after his furious contest, raised his eyes to the bull, and seemed to assent to the proposition. But alas! Man, cruel man, more brutal than the brutes themselves, would not permit them to carry out their pacific intentions. The two attendants and managers,

Ignacio and Gomez, stepped up behind them, goading them with spears until they again rushed upon each other, and fought with renewed desperation. During this scuffle, the bull shattered the lower jaw of the bear, and we could see the shivered bones dangling from their bloody recesses. Oh heaven what a horrible sight! How the blood curdled in my veins. Pish! What a timid fellow I am, to allow myself to be agitated by such a trifle as this! Shall I tremble at what the ladies applaud? Forbid it, Mars! I'll be as spirited as they. But to wind up this part of our story, neither the bull nor the bear could stand any longer—their limbs refused to support their bodies. They had worried and lacerated each other so much that their strength had completely failed, and they dropped upon the earth, gasping as if in the last agony. While in this helpless condition the chain was removed from their feet, horses were hitched to them and they were dragged without the arena, there to end their miseries in death.

During the California Gold Rush, which started at Sutter's Mill in 1848, about three hundred thousand people flooded into the state within a few years. The prospectors hunted for gold in the same thickly wooded river valleys where the grizzlies lived, and the bears were trapped and poisoned and shot on sight. In 1848 alone, five hunters delivered seven hundred grizzly bear pelts to the fort in Sacramento. The pelts, piled atop each other, reached to the top of the flagpole upon which flew the grizzly that had been adopted as the symbol of statehood. Ranchers, farmers, beekeepers and lumbermen followed in the wake of the miners, clearing land and killing any predators that hampered the march of civilization. In the summer, shepherds drove their sheep up the grassy slopes of the High Sierra, where the last populations of grizzly bears were holding out. Sheep, being fat and stupid, were a tempting target for bears, and the shepherds sowed strychnine-laced balls of tallow throughout the meadows. The poison killed anything that ate meat—coyotes, magpies, eagles, bobcats and grizzly bears, but that was all right because most wild animals, if not edible, were considered useless. Bears, in fact, were more valuable dead than alive since the State of California, the City of Santa Barbara and various cattlemen's associations paid a twenty-five dollar bounty for dead grizzly bears. A hunter named Ramon Ortega claimed to have killed forty grizzlies in thirty-five days, and to have lassoed and strangled seventy grizzly bears in five years. On his self-proclaimed best day, he killed fifteen. The San Luis Obispo *Tribune* confirmed that Ortega had two hundred grizzly bears "to his credit," half of which he had "strangled at the end of the riata, and equally as many he had killed with rifle or poison."

As the grizzlies dwindled, surviving individuals acquired a sort of outlaw infamy. Bears like Old Clubfoot and Slewfoot left distinctive tracks, thanks to run-ins with the massive steel traps manufactured, oddly enough, by the sexual libertines of the Oneida commune in rural New York state. But even these last notorious bears were pursued like stagecoach bandits. The Santa Ana Grizzly, alias Little Black Bear, was killed in 1908, and with its passing *Ursus arctos californicus* became extinct, except for its presence on the flag of California, on the football field and in other forums celebrating the indomitable spirit of the Golden Bear State. As the grizzly was making its last stand in California, the same war was being fought east of the Sierras, in the grasslands and range country of Montana and Wyoming and Colorado and the other western states.

In 1915 the outlaw bear that Seton made famous in his book *Biography of a Grizzly* was killed by a gentleman from Manhattan who owned a ranch in the hills of New Mexico and pursued the local bears whenever possible. Under the headline FAMOUS BEAR WAHB SLAIN, *The New York Times* announced that Meteetsee Wahb's "long career of pillage and slaughter was ended a few days ago by A.A. Anderson, who owns the ranch which made a home for the monster bear."

The newspaper enthused that Mr. Anderson had returned to his Manhattan home after a season of bear hunting with "Mayor Mitchel of New York." The report credited Anderson with killing "four bears this summer all on his ranch, a big one. The celebrated Wahb was one of the four. For years it had been the desire of Mr. Anderson to kill Wahb, but always before the cunning animal succeeded in outwitting the hunters."

In Utah a famous sheep-eating grizzly named Old Ephraim eluded hunters from 1911 until 1923. A reclusive trapper named Mr. Frank Clark kept trying to catch the bear, hiding huge leghold traps in mud wallows favoured by the grizzly. Each time, Ephraim would dig out the traps, spring them and throw them in the bush. Eventually, Mr. Clark planted a trap in a creek that Ephraim wasn't as familiar with, and managed to catch the giant bear by the front leg. The night the bear was caught, Clark was lying asleep in his bedroll about a mile from the trap set. He later wrote, "That night was fine, beautiful, a starlight night, and I was sleeping fine when I was awakened by a roar and a groan."

The grunting and chain-rattling noises became louder—it was Ephraim, coming to Mr. Clark's campsite to square accounts.

The bear had a big Oneida trap clamped to his front leg and was dragging a log at the end of a fourteen-foot logging chain.

Clark hurriedly put on "shoes but no trousers" and rushed out to meet the bear. It charged him on sight. He pumped seven rifle shots into the beast before it staggered and fell. When daylight came, he skinned the grizzly and buried the remains. Some local Boy Scouts later dug up the well-rotted skull, which they carried from a long pole because "it stunk like mad." It eventually ended up on display at Utah State University as a splendid example of *Ursus horribilis,* the so-called "horrible bear," which, thanks to an even more fearsome species, no longer inhabits Utah.

The Boy Scouts got a twenty-five dollar reward for turning in the skull, and Mr. Clark was celebrated for his diligence in hunting down the famous sheep-killer. In his account of the showdown, Mr. Clark remembered the awesome image of the bear as it stood up and attempted to charge him. He said the heavy trap chain was "wound around his right arm as carefully as a man would have done it, and a twenty-three-pound bear trap was on his foot. Standing nine feet, eleven inches tall, the bear was the most magnificent sight that any man could ever see."

Despite the fame that resulted from his killing of the bear, Mr. Clark was guilt-ridden for the rest of his life. Old Ephraim was the last grizzly in that part of Utah, and with the bear's death, something wild and free had been scrubbed from the landscape. "If I had it to do over again I wouldn't do it," Mr. Clark once confessed to his niece. Near the spot where he killed Ephraim, a monument the same height of the bear marks its grave.

By 1920 or so the plains grizzly was extinct. The hundred thousand grizzlies that had ranged throughout the lower United States only a century before had been reduced to one thousand, with most of those hiding out in the mountains of the western half of the continent. Alaska still had a good population of grizzlies, as did Canada—though the Canadian population of grizzlies was confined to rugged areas of the mountains of Alberta, British Columbia, the Yukon and the northern barrens. Although they are the masters of their close environment, grizzlies don't do well under pressure. Females don't mate until they are six years old, and even a healthy sow in her sexual prime may only have cubs every three years. Starvation, car accidents, rock slides, wolves, broken bones, parasites, disease and predatory large male grizzlies form a long and difficult gauntlet that a young bear must run to reach adulthood, and most don't make it.

Grizzlies did very well in pre-European North America because their adult mortality rate was so low. But in twentieth-century North America, even refuges like Yellowstone and Banff National Park had a hard time keeping healthy populations of bears. Poorly managed dumps created garbage-addicted bears that eventually got into trouble and needed to be destroyed. Grizzlies were hit with monotonous regularity on highways. They gravitated to railway tracks to feed on spilled grain and were killed by locomotives. Lodges, golf courses and ski resorts sprang up in the same lower valleys that the bears had used for millennia as foraging zones and travel corridors. On the coast of British Columbia, where prime forage and the annual salmon run supported far more bears than any other province in Canada, grizzlies still existed in moderate numbers. But as if aware of their threatened status, they only moved about under cover of darkness and usually fled at a whiff of mankind. You could go to places in prime bear country along the B.C. coast and see tracks. But it wasn't easy to find the animal that made them. On a fishing trip to the central coast of B.C., I once spent the better part of a morning with a local helicopter pilot, flying up and down mountain valleys, cruising feeder creeks and mud flats along the ocean and hovering at treetop level along rivers where salmon carcasses were littered by the thousands along the gravel bars. There were lots of black bears in evidence. But even though it was early September and the height of the salmon run, there didn't seem to be a grizzly in the entire country.

In the 1970s public attitudes about wild animals began to change. The environmental movement was gathering force, and citizens were beginning to place a higher value on wilderness and wildlife. Outdoor hobbies like rock climbing, canoeing and hiking were becoming popular, and animals like grizzly bears were seen as threatened symbols of the vanishing wilderness. More importantly, the prosperity of the post-war period afforded the scientific community the resources and the technological know-how to measure bear populations. Idealistic young biologists were hitting the field and coming back with studies that proved grizzlies were disappearing from many of their last strongholds, and human behaviour, more than habitat loss, was the demonstrable cause.

In 1975, under the provisions of the Endangered Species Act, the United States Fish and Wildlife Service designated the grizzly bear as a threatened species in the lower forty-eight states, and grizzly bear hunting was outlawed in Montana (Wyoming and Idaho had already closed their hunting seasons). In western Canada, excessive hunting, poaching, habitat loss due to sprawling human settlement and a general intolerance for big, dangerous animals had likewise caused a steep decline in grizzly populations. But hunting seasons were tightened up, dumps were cleaned up and strung with electric fencing, "bear-smart" education programs were introduced to reduce conflicts between bears and people, and, in parks like Banff, wildlife overpasses were built to allow grizzlies and other animals to cross busy highways without getting hit by vehicles. Slowly, the bears began to recover.

It's very hard to conduct a census of grizzlies, given that they live in extremely rugged country and are disinclined to be interviewed. Scientists use various means of measuring their populations, including extrapolating numbers from known populations and stringing barbed wire on trees to snag hair samples, which can then be subject to DNA analysis. These studies indicate that bear populations—both grizzly and black bears—are now recovering across much of western Canada. People who spend their lives in the bush—surveyors, prospectors, loggers and the like—say they are encountering more bears than ever. And statistics measuring property damage by bears, attacks on humans by bears, and bears destroyed by game wardens and police are on the rise.

Environmentalists distrust these numbers, mainly because of their effect; they argue that any talk of a "recovery" in grizzly bear populations will only encourage logging companies, miners, pro-hunting groups and governments to reintroduce policies that put the bears in trouble in the first place. Whatever the politics of the issue, scientists estimate that there are now about sixteen thousand grizzlies in British Columbia, which represents about 83 per cent of the saturation limit of the environment.

The crisis, in other words, is past. Or at least it is past in many parts of Canada and Alaska. Nowadays, if you're out walking in the bush, there has never been a more opportune time in recent history to come face to face with a grizzly bear.

Gary Shelton
and the Peaceable
Kingdom

Ifirst heard of Gary Shelton a few years ago, when I was having some breakfast, listening to CBC Radio and getting ready to pick up my shovel and walk to the mine, which in my case is a laptop computer around the corner from my dining room. The radio host was setting up one of those "panel discussions" in which people with antagonistic viewpoints are hauled into the studio, prodded with sticks and made to fight. In one corner was a scientist from the University of Alberta named Dr. Stephen Herrero. In another corner—or actually, on a crackly phone connection from Bella Coola, B.C.—was a backwoodsman named Gary Shelton.

Dr. Herrero is a specialist in wildlife ecology and a past president of the International Association for Bear Research. He is also the author of a book called *Bear Attacks: Their Causes and Avoidance,* a scrupulously researched study of bear-human conflict that has sold tens of thousands of copies across North America and was once selected by other scientists as "the most important scientific work on bears in the past twenty-five years." As an academic, he was dressed in white trunks as the sober defender of environmental principles and modern science.

Shelton was brought in to represent the rural, right-wing, gun-toting redneck constituency. As a former hunting guide, self-educated bear expert and outspoken debunker of "deliberate misinformation spread by certain members of the scientific community," Shelton appeared to be a perfect opponent for Herrero. He has written his own books about bear safety and bear attacks—books that are disliked by some environmentalists—so the confrontation seemed to offer all kinds of potential. To the chagrin of the CBC Radio host, however, the combatants refused to fight. They in fact seemed respectful of each other and cautiously concurred on key issues like bear population, bear hunting as a management tool and the many and varied causes of bear attacks. They also agreed that grizzlies have certain kinds of aggressive behaviours that are genetically programmed and serve bears well when it comes to defending their food, protecting their offspring and prevailing over other animals. Their key point seemed to be that when people get attacked by bears, it's not necessarily because the person has done something wrong. Bears sometimes attack people because that's what bears do.

Shelton argued that a closely regulated hunting season is a good thing for a number of reasons: bear populations are reduced in overcrowded areas, the surviving bears are therefore larger, stronger and healthier, and most importantly, hunted bears avoid humans. What really caught my attention was the evidence he cited to prove his point. He said that he knew of five different homes in Bella Coola where large, dominant grizzly bears regularly bed down during the daytime within a hundred and fifty yards of those homes, yet because these bears have been educated by hunters and are therefore wary of humans, the home owners there never see them. He said he lives in a modern home near Bella Coola with a highway going past his front door, but for four months every year, there isn't a night when grizzlies don't cross his property, and an eight-hundred-pound dominant male grizzly often beds down under a tree on the edge of his backyard. He said that so far, the proximity of these bears hasn't been a problem because grizzlies in Bella Coola have been trained to lie low in daylight hours and generally avoid people. But he warned that as hunting seasons are cut back, the bear population is increasing and attacks on people will be inevitable.

I walked across the room and turned up the radio, in fear that the dishwasher would start up or a jet airplane would pass over the house or something else would happen that would prevent me from hearing every single word of the interview. I had read so many books over the years that portray the grizzly as an animal that needs vast tracts of untouched wilderness—an animal so wild and majestic it simply can't tolerate human beings and is in fact disgusted by our smell—that I was having a hard time believing what I was hearing. My mind was awhirl with envy. Why couldn't I have an eight-hundred-pound male grizzly bedded down under a fir tree in my backyard?

Later on that same day, I purchased Herrero's book and sent away for Shelton's books and found them to be gripping reading—a blend of nature lore, philosophy and hair-raising accounts of bear attacks. The idea of returning to Bella Coola kept playing on my mind, and a year after hearing Gary Shelton interviewed on CBC Radio, I flew out to Vancouver on a lovely September day, transferred to a little turbo-prop and headed north to Bella Coola. The coastal mountains were white-capped and radiant in the afternoon sun, but by the time we reached Bella Coola the coastal range was blanketed with heavy cloud. Here and there a spire of rock rose from the cotton. The pilot announced that it was clearer to the east, so we flew over to Anahim Lake, landed, dropped a few people off, then made another attempt to descend into Bella Coola, this time flying beneath the ceiling, with the steep walls of the narrow valley going past on either side of the plane. There were only half a dozen passengers onboard and they must have been locals, because they thumbed through their magazines in a half-interested way as the stone massifs paraded by the window. I passed the time looking for goats and wondering whether kerosene explodes on impact or merely dribbles down the rock face. Then we glided down into the Bella Coola Valley and landed at the airport with a pleasant slam and a roar of engines.

There are no taxis in Bella Coola, so I hitched a ride with a local fellow to the Bay Motor Hotel, a modest two-storey building on the side of the highway a couple of miles up the valley. When I made my travel plans, I had cold-called Gary Shelton and asked if I could buy him dinner, and although he didn't know me from Adam, he had agreed to meet me at the hotel around six this evening. It was only mid-afternoon, so I checked into my room and

took a walk up the highway, breathing the pine-freshened air, surveying the misty mountaintops and marvelling that everything still
looked familiar after all these years.

A mile from the hotel, a shallow feeder creek scuffled under
the bridge. The skeletons of dead salmon were scattered in the
shallows. There are five main types of salmon in the Pacific, and
they spawn in stages, each subspecies waiting its turn to die.
These carcasses looked like pink salmon, and I climbed down the
bank to look at them. For a while I walked up the creek. It was
hard to hunt for tracks because the ground was paved with loose
stones. I wasn't much worried about bears because trucks were
thundering across the bridge right behind me, and in any case I
was accustomed to looking for grizzlies and never finding them.
But when I reached the elbow bend of the creek, the sound of
the traffic faded behind me and I began to feel uneasy. On every
river there's a sort of foyer where you feel yourself stepping from
the new world into the primeval one. Since the only weapon in
my possession was a pocket comb, I decided to swap ends and
head back to the hotel.

I had assumed that Gary Shelton would telephone me
from the front desk when he arrived, but by six-fifteen there
was still no call, and by six-thirty I was concerned enough to
call his house, where there was no answer. Had I gotten the
date wrong? I went down to the restaurant, talked to the waitress and discovered, to my chagrin, that Shelton had been waiting all this time by himself in the restaurant and had just given
up and left. I called his house again and caught him as he was
coming in the door. He was forgiving about my mistake and
agreed to drive all the way back to the hotel, so I sat down to
wait for him. When he entered the restaurant, I knew it was

him, even though I had never seen his picture and had no idea what he looked like. It's a cliché to observe that people who study wild animals come to physically resemble their subjects, but Gary Shelton really does look like he's inherited a grizzly gene or two. Tall and wide-shouldered, with tufted eyebrows and a face that looks fierce even in composure, Shelton padded into the room and introduced himself with the deferential manners of a man who knows he looks formidable.

After we'd talked a bit and ordered dinner, he told me that, like many others, he heard about Bella Coola Valley when he was a young man in the United States and fell in love with it upon his first visit. He moved here in the 1960s, worked as a hunting guide and spent many years travelling and camping out in remote places where he learned about nature by observation and experience. In the 1970s he became concerned that grizzly bear populations were dwindling because of overhunting, habitat destruction and other kinds of excess, and he threw himself into volunteer work to raise awareness of the importance of bear conservation. He became chairman of the Central Coast Grizzly Management Committee, an influential group made up of government representatives and other parties interested in bear conservation. They tightened up hunting laws, introduced regulations to reduce the nuisance bear kill and moved to protect high-value bear habitat.

By 1985 the province was managing bears in a more effective way, and grizzly populations across the province began to recover. But as the old saying goes, be careful what you wish for. The age-old relationship between people and bears is a troubled one, and as the grizzly population in B.C. increased, attacks on livestock and people also increased. Forestry workers and surveyors were running into more bears, and employers were getting nervous about safety and liability issues. "By the late 1980s I had experienced over a hundred close-up encounters with grizzlies and black bears," Shelton told me as he drank his coffee. "People knew that I had spent a lot of time observing bears and studying their behaviour, and they often asked me for advice. There was a lot of misinformation on the subject of bear safety, so I began giving people advice, and this evolved into a training package."

In 1989 the Ministry of Forests called him and asked him to conduct a series of bear-safety training programs for its forestry workers. He says his courses were very hands-on and practical, focusing on bear behaviour, bear conflict avoidance and self-defence. The program was popular with the students, and he still has file drawers full of letters from graduates who feel that his training helped them extricate themselves from sticky situations. The word got around, and other government ministries began calling him up for training sessions. By the 1990s his bear safety lessons had become a full-time job, keeping him travelling back and forth across the province, teaching courses to everyone from college students who'd never seen a bear in their life to park wardens with half a lifetime on the job. In 1994 he published his first book, *Bear Encounter Survival Guide.* The book was based on his training program, and it quickly became a widely distributed safety manual for bush workers across B.C. and Alaska. His second book was more controversial. *Bear Attacks: The Deadly Truth* came out after he'd spent several years researching bear fatalities and interviewing people who'd been horribly maimed by bears.

His ideas are controversial because, among other things, Shelton argues that bears are now too abundant and need to be trimmed back. He advocates hunting as the best way of keeping populations in check and suggests that a gun and diligent practice with a gun are the safest means of personal defence when travelling or working in grizzly country. At the heart of his book is the argument that people and bears are historic antagonists and always will be. This may seem like a rather harmless and even interesting philosophical take, but it touches a nerve in the environmental movement, where conflicts are invariably blamed on people, and guns and no-nonsense attitudes about bears are seen as part of the problem rather than the solution. As an illustration of this, when I was trying to find Gary Shelton's books, I called several different mountain bookstores in British Columbia and was informed by the owners that they didn't carry his books because of what one store manager confidentially described as "the content." I asked her what she meant, and she confessed that she hadn't actually read his books but had received "complaints from some of our regular customers."

I thought this was a little excessive. After all, we weren't exactly talking about *Mein Kampf* here. But store owners, one accepts, are entitled to sell whatever books they choose, so I went to a backup source, the Internet, and during that search process I stumbled across book reviews like this one, posted on the website of the Raincoast Conservation Society: "Shelton is a grizzly killer and has written a sensationalist anti-science piece of crap book that demonizes large carnivores and is essentially a rationalization for continuing to kill grizzlies, wolves, etc. in BC for fun and profit."

All this negativity only served to make me more curious about Shelton's books, which, as it turned out, contain little that is particularly inflammatory or dangerous. Even if you disagree with him—and many well-qualified scientists do—it seems a little Orwellian to deal with an author's opinions by suppressing his books. Shelton looked amused when I told him about his evident unpopularity with book retailers and environmental activists like the Raincoast Conservation Society. "A lot of people out there hate me," he admitted. "I would love to have the opportunity to debate them, but they usually avoid me. They don't think anyone who disagrees with them should have the right to speak."

He went on to argue that the "preservationist" movement, as opposed to the "conservationist" movement, has spread a lot of misinformation about grizzlies. "Bears, like all animals, are driven by simple self-interest. And that's how they've survived for tens of thousands of years. You can only coexist with a bear by giving it what it wants. You have to do things the bear's way. If your fruit trees attract bears, you only have limited choices—you can either give the bear free access to the fruit or you get rid of the trees. Last year, one of our local old-timers was attacked by a grizzly right in his front yard. Some 'bear expert' from the university told the media it was his own fault for having fruit trees in his yard. Well, a lot of people who live in rural areas don't necessarily have a lot of money and they can't afford to get rid of their fruit trees just because some environmentalist in Vancouver thinks that bears should have more rights than we do."

I confessed that I had never seen a grizzly and that that was one of the reasons I had come back to Bella Coola.

He thought about this for a moment, then looked at his watch and asked the waitress, "Did you put our dinner on the grill yet?"

She said she hadn't.

He looked at me. "Do you want to take a little drive? Maybe we can find one."

I couldn't think of anything I would rather do. We climbed into his truck and drove up the valley. The landscape on either side of the road was rainforest interspersed here and there with pasture land, horse corrals and little ranch homes. It looked peaceful, but Shelton said it was not an easy place to live off the land. The Norwegians who pioneered these homesteads had to cope with isolation, rough winters and constant struggles with wild animals. "You hear people talk about coexisting peacefully with bears, but that's an urban concept. If you live in the city, and you just want to come up here and look at bears, then yes, you can coexist peacefully with them. But if you live here year round, and you raise your own livestock and garden produce, you are inevitably going to have conflicts with grizzly bears."

As we drove slowly through the dusky light, Shelton looked to the left and right, eyeing the forest edges and mountain slopes. Ten minutes after we'd left the hotel, he abruptly slowed the truck. "There's one."

He eased the truck onto the shoulder and pointed into a hay-field. I couldn't see anything at first, but followed his gesture to a spot about a hundred yards away where two small objects were protruding from the high grass and slowly moving sideways—a pair of ears.

"Get out of the truck very quietly and don't slam the door."

I climbed out and made my way to his side of the vehicle, where he had quietly closed his door. We stood on the highway watching the two small ears moving through the alfalfa.

"Stay next to me and do exactly as I say."

The two objects slowly resolved into the vague profile of a bear's head, neck and upper shoulders. The breeze was in our favour and we hadn't made a sound, but the bear nevertheless somehow became aware of our presence and stood up, revealing itself to be as tall as a man. The grizzly's head swivelled from side to side as it scanned the landscape. Despite the common misconception that bears are almost blind, they can see as well as humans. When its eyes locked on us it flinched as if it had nosed a hotwire. It woofed, dropped to all fours, took a few quick lateral strides and stood up again.

"Don't move."

This was the moment of truth, the moment when a wild grizzly evaluates the situation and decides whether to act offensively or defensively. The bear galloped a few feet sideways, then stood up again, weaving its head back and forth. We don't normally think of animals as capable of "thought," but even at this distance it was clear the bear was trying to figure us out. Dropping to all fours, it retreated for the tall timber, its huge bulk moving in a fluid rocking-horse canter.

"See, that's what I want a grizzly to do," Shelton said. "That bear was raised properly by its mother. I've seen mother grizzly bears teach their cubs about humans. She'll start woofing and the cubs will run around in little circles, squalling in fear because they know Mama is upset and might give them a smack. A young bear never forgets the lessons it learns from its mother. If it's taught to fear humans it will always avoid humans, and that's good for the bear and good for the people it meets."

We went back to the hotel for dinner, and the next day he took me to his home, a stylish and comfortable ranch house at the base of a mountain, surrounded by an immense lawn and well-kept gardens. Inside his house, framed photos and big-game trophies compete for wall space with books by classical philosophers like Plato, Descartes and Karl Marx, and modern essayists like Herbert Marcuse, Aldo Leopold and Barry Lopez. "I spent ten years reading books like these on my own, studying the history of Western thought and educating myself in philosophy. Rural values were just starting to come under attack by preservationists, and I felt I needed to make myself familiar with the great thinkers and study logic so that I could step forward and debate these people. Somebody had to take them on, so I did. But I don't know if it helped much, because they won in the end. Their support base is urban, and that's where the votes are, so the government knuckled under and gave them what they wanted. Our logging and hunting have more or less been shut down. Our young people have left town to look for jobs in the city. Our community is in deep recession. But the bears have done all right. We're starting to encounter bold, day-active grizzlies all over the place. You might envy us having all these bears around, but when you live here, it's not so great. Local mothers are afraid to let their kids play outside. A fellow up the road had his ten-thousand-dollar roping horse killed by a bear. My neighbour looked out the window the other day and there was a grizzly walking up her driveway. It's getting to the point in this valley that it's not really safe to be outside without protection."

Loading a rifle and clipping two large canisters of bear spray to his belt, Shelton offers to take me for a walk. He hands me a large canister of pepper spray and shows me how to use it. Outside, the September sun is shining on the mountaintop and the cottonwoods in the lowlands are showing patches of gold. A wolf howls up on the mountain. You don't often hear wolves calling in the middle of the day, but this one no sooner empties his chest than it lets go again, a clear, long lament that echoes down the valley. We walk across Shelton's yard to his horse corral, where he's installed a sort of pet door in the rail fencing. It looks like an oversize version of the crawlway they put in the chain-link fence at a schoolyard. "The grizzlies used to knock the fence down when they came through the yard," says Shelton. "I'd repair it and they'd knock it down again. So I built this gate for them and they learned to use it. They come through here every night. I can tell when a bear is crossing the property because the dog challenges them with a distinctive bark."

We walk across the lawn to the edge of the woods and a big cedar tree, where he shows me a scraped-up patch of ground. "Do you know what this is?" he asks.

"No."

"It's a grizzly bear's bed," he says. "There's a salmon stream running right through the woods there. A big male grizzly often beds down here in the daytime, within sight of my kitchen window. He's bluff-charged me a few times, but we've worked out a truce. Still, you'd be very foolish to walk anywhere around here without a gun or pepper spray."

Shelton leads me into the woods, walking point a few steps ahead of me, periodically shouting, "Hey bear, hey bear!" to warn any bedded grizzlies of our approach. He explains there are two dangerous scenarios in these woods: surprising a sow with young cubs, or walking up on an adult grizzly bedded down by a food cache. Most other grizzlies will retreat if they are given the opportunity. Shelton always makes a lot of noise as he moves through cover and walks downwind so the bears can detect his approach well ahead of time. His rifle has open sights and is chambered for the formidable .358 Norma magnum. For safety reasons he always carries it with an empty chamber, but has practised with it so much he can cycle a round into the chamber and fire an accurate shot in less than a second.

Not everyone is comfortable with guns or comfortable with Shelton's assertion that a firearm in the hands of a competent handler is the best life insurance in grizzly country. But all the same, it's a rare forestry scientist or bear biologist or eco-guide who doesn't pack a gun. All you need to see is the full-out charge of a grizzly on video to appreciate the extraordinary passion of the bear's attack. Even watching a film, you feel stunned and a little confused by the animal's disproportionate fury, the charge unfolding so rapidly the film has to be slowed down before you can see the bear—a blurry cannonball of fur exploding through the undergrowth towards the camera. The safety books say that the worst thing you can do is run, but even trained scientists tend to crap their pants when they see that ball of fury blasting through the brush towards them.

In his training courses, Shelton teaches advanced gun-handling tactics to non-hunters (forestry workers, surveyors and the like). Hunters don't take his courses because they don't think they need them. But Shelton says even the most seasoned hunters can find they're not as deft and accurate with a gun as they thought they were, especially when the situation is complicated by the panic and adrenaline of a real-life bear attack. Shelton has fired thousands of rounds in practice at moving targets, dealt with many charging grizzlies at close range, and tells me that from a statistical point of view, a firearm still provides better odds of survival than pepper spray or other tools. "A person who has trained sufficiently with a firearm can reduce their chance of injury or death in a bear encounter to about nil."

As he explains all this, we're walking through a logged-over forest, which is jammed up now with herbaceous second growth and tangled underbrush. Pointing out well-worn bear trails, droppings and berry bushes, he says wild animals such as moose, deer, bear and cougar love these cutovers. They're a smorgasbord of plant foods. "When a logging operation or a fire takes out the big trees, the sun gets in and there's rampant growth of rosehips, berries and all kinds of other forage. They've done radio-collar studies that show bears prefer cutover areas, and every scientist knows that. But if you want to drive an environmentalist crazy, just say that logging is good for wild animals."

Farther down the trail, we enter a primeval rainforest, a section of old growth that Shelton and some of his friends saved from logging many years ago. "You need a mix of old growth and new growth in any healthy forest. These are ancient trees, and you'll notice there's very little bear sign. I don't love logging. In fact, I've been very active at curtailing excessive logging in this valley. But it's ridiculous to argue that protecting old growth is equivalent to protecting wildlife."

Later we walk back to his house and we go for a drive up the valley. At one spot, he stops the truck and takes me for a walk into the bush to see an ancient campsite. It's an overhanging rock ledge once used as a shelter by pre-contact aboriginals, with a large rock painting of a sow grizzly on the wall. Even in this crude sketch, there's no mistaking the menace in her posture. She's standing with her cub at her side and her claws drooping like Freddy Krueger's in *Nightmare on Elm Street*. The rock overhang is still smudged with soot from the campfire, making it seem as if the people who camped here left only a few weeks ago. In fact, in archaeological terms, it wasn't long ago when this valley was occupied only by Stone-Age aboriginals, people who must have been extraordinarily brave and tenacious to challenge grizzlies and other big predators for the right to live here.

"That petroglyph reveals a lot about what a fearsome rival the grizzly bear must have been," says Shelton. "I was at a bear conference a few years ago, and this scientist got up and said, 'Native people lived in peace with bears for ten thousand years—why can't we?' You hear that all the time, but it's a myth. The native people never lived in peace with bears. Just ask the native elders themselves. Go into the libraries and read the ethnologies. They were in constant conflict with bears. They feared them and avoided them and killed them whenever they could. In this valley, the Nuxalk people set snares and deadfalls on the trails and suppressed the bear population to well below what it is now. The grizzlies were dangerous and the natives didn't want them around. If you read Alexander Mackenzie's journal, he came across the mountains and down this valley on foot two centuries ago and never saw a single grizzly."

The next day we encounter more grizzlies, but these live in Tweedsmuir Park, about an hour's drive up the valley from Bella Coola. Shelton has brought me here to demonstrate that park bears behave differently from wild bears. When we cross the boundary into the park, right away we start seeing grizzlies. But they're park grizzlies, and it's debatable whether park grizzlies are real grizzlies. Shelton pulls into a campground and parks the vehicle, and we walk down to the banks of the Atnarko River, where a sow grizzly and her cubs are fishing in the shallows about fifty yards downstream of the campground. They ignore us, and they ignore a rubber raft that drifts by with some ecotourists in it. Sitting down on a park bench, we watch the mother bear and her cubs for a while. Then a large male grizzly emerges from the undergrowth on the other side of the river, maybe twenty yards away. The water between us is shallow, and we're well inside his personal space. But you can tell by his body language that he's not paying us the slightest heed. He just sniffs the water and walks on down the riverbank. "He knows we're here," murmurs Shelton. "But he doesn't care." Farther down the river, we see a small sub-adult grizzly cutting through the shallows, splashing past a fisherman with a fly rod. The angler stands there looking stiff and uneasy as the bear wallows past.

"These are habituated grizzlies," says Shelton. "They don't mind people as long as the people don't get in their way. It looks very safe, but the arrangement can turn dangerous quickly. This campground is an accident waiting to happen. Sooner or later some naive tourist is going to get jumped by one of these bears, and then there will be all this hand-wringing about the 'unpredictable' nature of bears. They're not unpredictable at all. Bears are inherently aggressive went it comes to food. They compete with each other by intimidation and, if necessary, brute force. They'll suddenly attack each other over a scrap of food, and if they lose their fear of people, they will treat people the same way. So you wouldn't want to camp here. If one of these bears decided to have a look inside your tent in the middle of the night, you'd have a very dangerous situation on your hands."

With the bear at a safe distance, the fisherman once again starts canvassing the river with his fly rod. His line loops out and pops a corona of fine mist as it straightens and descends. The bear sits on its rump in the shallows, idly watching him cast. It's late afternoon, warm and pleasant, and the sun is gilding the river with September light. It looks like the Peaceable Kingdom, the grizzly bear and the man sharing the river, but I'm not sure what will happen if he hooks a fish, or to what extent I'm seeing what I would like to see as opposed to what's actually occurring. There were probably scenes like this occurring every day in Glacier Park before it all went wrong.

As we're watching, the underbrush rustles and a large creature comes clawing its way up the riverbank towards us. My heart
revs until the creature emerges from the undergrowth and turns
out to be a person, thank God—a sturdy, blonde-haired tourist
with a telephoto-equipped camera looped around her neck. A
moment later her husband appears, chattering gaily in German,
pointing across the river to the bear sitting on its rump in the shallows. They've spotted the photo opportunity and they're excited
to get a photo. Deploying their cameras, they clamber through
the riverbank undergrowth towards the young grizzly.

Throughout all this, Gary doesn't say anything. But I can
tell by his silence he doesn't approve of what he's seeing. When
the noise started coming up the bank towards us he didn't flinch.
Maybe he knew they weren't bears. Or perhaps he's just inherently that vigilant. He brought a large canister of pepper spray,
and ever since we arrived he's been carrying it in his hand.

Tilley Hats
and Armed Security

The growth in bear populations along the west coast hasn't been a worry for everyone. Some individuals have learned to make a buck out of it. A few hundred miles north of Vancouver, a clutter of mountainous islands blocks the top end of the Georgia Strait. The clefts and passages here are so narrow in places that the tides churn through at eighteen knots, generating torrents that kick up spray like the Colorado River. For millennia, these passes have played host to a large migration of Chinook salmon. The fish poured down through the tangle of islands and nosed their way up into the coastal rivers to spawn. Nowadays, thanks to avaricious commercial fishermen and hog-stupid federal politicians, there are hardly any Chinook salmon left.

The big chrome Chinooks may be almost gone, but the grizzly bears are back. They no doubt miss the Chinooks as much as the rest of us, but they seem to do just fine on the little hooknosed pink salmon that still flood into the coastal rivers every summer. Many of the fishing lodges along the west coast have been forced by the decline of the much-desired Chinook to promote other activities besides fishing. A lot of them are trying to bring in business groups for "team-building getaways." Some of the fancier ones are installing therapy rooms, massage tables and the like and trying to sell themselves as remote spas for the wealthy. Others are promoting this hot new industry: ecotourism. The idea is that, instead of going out trolling for the king of fishes, you can go out trolling for the king of bears, with a camera instead of a fishing rod.

A year after my trip to Bella Coola, I flew up to Sonora Island with my girlfriend's son, Nick, to see if we could see some grizzlies. Nick is a talented young photographer, and I hoped he'd get some nice shots for his art program in Chicago and maybe bag me a good grizzly portrait for my office wall. Privately, I hoped we'd also have an experience like my first one with Gary Shelton, an unmediated electroshock encounter with a bona fide wild grizzly, but closer.

At the Fraser River seaplane base in Vancouver, we boarded a turbo Beaver and flew north over the rumpled green mountains of the west coast to Sonora Resort, which is now much fancier than it used to be, with a swish dining room, elegant store, business centre, fitness facility, tennis dome and pathways winding off to the sort of elegant suites where you find soft music playing and an organic chocolate on the pillow when you come in after dinner. Old fishermen say the fancier the fishing lodge, the smaller the fish, and there does seem to be an inverse relationship between depleted resources and the availability of excellent cuisine. After going out the first day and catching a few small pink salmon, we don survival suits on the morning of day two and board a large yellow Zodiac inflatable with about a dozen other guests and sally off in search of grizzly bears.

It's a stunningly beautiful morning. The water is smooth and the mountainous shoreline on either side of Bute Inlet rises up in cloud-wreathed palisades. We are wearing headphones so we can listen to the comments of our eco-guide, who is going to teach us about what we are seeing. The typical modern eco-tour evokes memories of a Grade 7 field trip, with your most well-meaning and humourless science teacher narrating facts about nature as you cruise past eagle nests and other material from the curriculum. Halfway up the inlet, a small pod of Pacific white-sided dolphins appear in the distance, skipping like bombs on the mirrored sea, and when they spot us they change course and come racing towards us, body surfing in our wake and dodging back and forth in front of the boat.

At the mouth of the Orford River, we pull up to a pier where a couple of eco-guides from the local Homalco First Nation are waiting for us. The guides, James Hacket and Ben Wilson, lead us to a battered old school bus with "Welcome to Grizzly Country" emblazoned on the side. We climb in and bounce through the forest for a mile or so. Taciturnity is a valued trait in native culture, and the young men aren't much interested in treating us in the sycophantic manner of typical tour guides. But they seem to enjoy their work and they exchange muttered witticisms with each other as the bus lurches through the dark, moss-drooping rainforest. Hacket tells me that bear-watching has created good, steady jobs for his band. He and about ten other Homalco people work here from May to November, and in an average year they take five hundred tourists to look at the bears. "We teach people about our culture too. Like, our word for the grizzly is *xawges*. The black bear is *maxalth*."

At the end of the road, Ben parks the bus. James removes a couple of pump-action 12-gauge shotguns from their cases and hands one to Ben. "We're going to check to make sure it's safe to go outside," James says. As he opens the door and descends the stairs, he sends us a deadpan look. "If we don't come back, the keys are in the ignition."

When James and Ben have ascertained that the coast is clear, we troop out of the bus and walk in orderly summer-camp formation to a wooden staircase leading up to a viewing platform. It's basically a treehouse overlooking a broad stretch of braided rapids. A few half-dead salmon are struggling in the shallows. There are no bears in sight. But after a few minutes, as if on cue, a chalky-brown grizzly comes out of the bush on the far side of the river and walks through the shallows, nosing a few dying salmon before selecting one and carrying it up onto the gravel to eat. Wolves and grizzlies are not as large as you might think. These grizzlies have a lot of salmon to eat, so they are allegedly amongst the largest in North America, but still, a typical one is about the size of an oil drum on stubby legs. There is indeed such a thing as an "enormous grizzly," just as there is such a thing as an "enormous human," but the typical grizzly is, like a movie star, smaller than you'd expect. Over the next half hour other grizzly bears come and go, and the machine drives of the many cameras whir each time one appears. Nick has a good telephoto lens and says he is getting some great shots. The quieter of our two guides,

Wilson, leans up against the wall with his shotgun in his arms, looking like a bank guard not averse to exchanging small talk with the customers. "Lots of bears here this year," he tells me.

"More than last year?"

"Yep."

"More than when you were a kid?"

"There's way more nowadays," he says. "We hardly ever saw grizzlies when I was a kid."

"Why?"

"People used to kill them."

"Native people or white people?"

"Everybody killed them."

"Why?"

"People didn't want them around. Even in the old days, before there was guns, our people would go up on the mountain where the bears were sleeping. They'd build a fire and blow the smoke into the den. When the bear came out, they'd throw big rocks down on him."

Ben Wilson seems like such a mild-tempered fellow that it's hard to imagine him killing a mouse, let alone a bear. I ask him if they've ever had to shoot a bear, and he nods. "Just one," he says. "Back in the 1990s. You get a bad bear once in a while, but this system works pretty well."

We lean against the railing in silence for a while, watching the grizzlies. One of the tourists is aiming a long telephoto lens at the cliff across the valley. The morning sun is gilding the rocks and an eagle is soaring above it. "That's Lookout Point," Ben tells him. "In the old days, a couple of our people would camp out on that cliff and keep watch."

"What were they watching for?"

"Other Indians," he says.

"Why?"

"They'd raid our villages for slaves."

"Which tribe took the slaves?"

"All of them. They'd come and take our children and women."

So much for life in Eden. At the next stop, we climb off the bus and walk down a trail alongside the river. James walks at the end of the line and Ben leads the group. I ask James, "What do you recommend doing if we meet a grizzly?"

"Pee your pants."

"Some people say you're supposed to act submissively."

"I don't agree with that."

"Why not?"

"Then you're telling him he's the boss."

Ben weighs in. "One time I was walking this trail without my gun, and I came face to face with a big grizzly."

"What did you do?"

"You know how a grizzly clicks his teeth together to show the other bear who's the boss? I picked up two rocks and clicked them together, and he stepped into the river to let me go by."

"That was a smart thing to do."

"It worked that time, anyway."

A few hundred yards farther, we reach a gravel flat where a creek enters the river. The river is quite deep, but the water so transparent the pebbled bottom looms up as if through a lens. Hundreds of red salmon jockey and turn in the insistent current. On the far side of the river, a hundred yards away, a sow grizzly stares at the surface of the river as if thinking. Two cubs tussle and romp nearby. One of them spots us and immediately starts squalling and dancing like a windup toy. "That cub, we call him Squawker," says Ben. "He's always making noise. I think he's going to be an aggressive bear when he grows up."

James nods. "He never shuts up. When they're back in the woods you can hear him from a long way off. The other one doesn't like to fish and gets his mother to do everything. We call him Moocher."

"They're all different," Ben concludes. "They're just like people."

Bear tours like the one the Homalco operate for Sonora Lodge are becoming more popular. In Alaska and down along the coast of British Columbia, numerous eco-tour companies specialize in taking people out to look at grizzly bears. You can live on a luxury sailboat and cruise the shorelines, or stay on a floating lodge that offers hot tubs and gourmet meals, or just climb aboard a small boat in some coastal community and take a day trip with a professional eco-guide to a nearby river where bears are fishing for salmon. In fact, the entire British Columbia coast from Vancouver Island to the Alaska panhandle is becoming one big bear-watching region, a sort of open-air zoo in which the visitors are essentially in cages instead of the bears.

It all started back in the 1990s, when rock stars, prominent environmental activists like Robert Kennedy Jr. and a wide coalition of young people, aging hippies, environmentalists and native leaders blocked the logging of a beautiful piece of old-growth rainforest on the west coast of Vancouver Island called Clayoquot Sound. Encouraged by that victory, the environmentalists set their sights on the mainland, where loggers were preparing to cut the giant trees that grow along a two-hundred-and-fifty-mile stretch of coast on either side of Bella Coola. Recognizing that every campaign needs a logo or a symbol of some kind—and a big old tree just isn't huggable enough—the environmentalists chose for their icon the Kermode bear, a type of black bear that, because of a recessive gene in its parents, is born white. There are only four or five hundred Kermode bears along the entire west coast, and their scarcity afforded them mystery and cachet.* Rebranding the Kermode bear as "the Spirit Bear," the activists designed a marketing campaign that encouraged tourists and visiting travel writers to believe that some kind of spiritual transformation happened to anyone who visited the area and was lucky enough to see one. The entire coastline was then renamed as "the Great Bear Rainforest," and it was strongly suggested that the survival of the pure white Spirit Bears and giant grizzlies was dependent on the preservation of the region's ancient trees.

The next step was dubbed "War in the Woods." With a combination of human blockades, guerrilla warfare and sophisticated international marketing campaigns, the environmental coalition took the battle to the seat of real power—the middle-class North American living room. More than eighty companies with an urban customer base—including massive retailers like Home Depot and Ikea—saw the writing on the wall and agreed to do their part to "save the bears" by boycotting lumber from old-growth forests. To shut down the hunting season, or at least to get a start on it, the Raincoast Conservation Society—the same group so enamoured

---

* It's not easy to get a look at a Kermode or Spirit Bear. Only one in ten of the local black bears is born white, so you have to work your way through a lot of black bears before glimpsing a white one. Despite the alleged harm that logging does to bear populations, one of the most reliable spots to see a Kermode bear is a former logging site on Gribble Island, north of Princess Royal Island, where local natives maintain a couple of viewing platforms overlooking a clearcut.

of Gary Shelton and his books—closed a $1 million deal with a local outfitter to buy out the hunting rights for nearly twenty thousand square miles of old growth coastline. (The Conservation Society has declared that it has no intention to use its territory for hunting. But that's a government prerequisite for holding the rights, so that deal may eventually run into trouble.) With the 2010 Olympics looming, the government of British Columbia got with the program and adopted the Spirit Bear as its official plush-toy mascot of the Winter Olympics.

So all up and down the central coast, the emphasis is now on old-growth preservation and non-consumptive tourism. Take nothing but pictures; leave nothing but footprints. Bear watching there is not yet as big as it is in northern Manitoba, where fifteen thousand visitors come to see polar bears every year and pump millions of dollars into the northern economy, but it's growing in that direction. And really, one doesn't have to be a rabid environmentalist to see the logic in saving some of the world's last rainforest and photographing bears instead of shooting them.

Still, marching around under armed guard with a crowd of tourists in Tilley hats is not quite what I had in mind when I hit the road with Dave more than thirty years ago. Back in those days, I imagined that locking eyes with a grizzly bear might offer some clue into the ancient cipher of life. I never expected that the grizzlies would walk around ignoring us. I had since been to some interesting places, and eyeballed several dozen grizzlies in various situations, but only one of those circumstances felt like an actual encounter— the wild grizzly that reared onto its back legs and shot a tense glance at Gary Shelton and me across a hundred yards of open field that evening in Bella Coola. That encounter lasted only a few seconds, but it was more interesting than all the others put together.

Grizzlies
Own the Night

A month after coming home from Bute Inlet, I decided to take one last trip to Bella Coola, this time travelling by boat up the coast—a smart decision, as it turned out, as there is no more pleasant a way to make your way up into the central coast, or, excuse me, the Great Bear Rainforest.

The word "ferry" evokes an image of a diesel-powered parking garage loaded with cars and Greyhound buses, but this particular boat, operated by B.C. Ferries, was a rakish white cruiser that was more of an ocean-going ship than a ferry. We set sail in the misty pre-dawn darkness of Port Hardy and spent the entire day cruising up the coast through narrow fjords and misty inlets. The first killer whales that surfaced a few hundred yards from the ship provoked a flurry of excitement from the passengers. But by mid-afternoon the few dozen of them on board (the crew outnumbered the passengers) had grown blasé, given that most of the time, whenever you looked across the sea you could see a whale or a pod of dolphins. At one point, an enormous humpback rose directly in the path of the ship and sank lazily as the captain blew the foghorn. For long moments the water spooled and eddied where the behemoth descended. In places, the passages were so narrow the passing mountain walls were only a hundred yards away, and in the fog that descended in the last half of the afternoon, broken cedars hung above the ship like the gargoyles of Notre Dame. It felt as though we were in a modern version of the journey to find King Kong.

Long after dark, after fourteen hours or so at sea, the ship approached Bella Coola. The captain sounded the foghorn, idled the engines and shot a lance of light across the black water. The pier was dark in the falling rain. A few headlights crept across the pier to give the skipper help in navigating. It had the feeling of arriving in a place that time had forgotten, and in many ways it was. Bella Coola is a smaller village now than it was when I first visited thirty years ago. Catching a ride, I checked into the Brockton Inn, a nice little guest house up the valley. Unpacking my bags, I charged the batteries for my camera and prepared to spend another week exploring the valley, talking to the locals, fly-fishing for coho and hoping to meet a wild grizzly at close range.

In the morning I walked to the hotel in Hagensborg and had breakfast in the restaurant. On the way the morning sun was dawning over the mountain ridge. There were a few unemployed loggers in the restaurant, old-timers with broken hands and lots of time to nurse their coffee and look out the window. In Bella

Coola, most of the lumberjacks are fourth- or fifth-generation Scandinavians. All their lives, they supported their families by clambering up and down steep mountain slopes and doing the second most dangerous job in North America. Like miners, high-steel riggers and other men who work a heartbeat away from death or dismemberment, the typical logger is not, as one might expect, a tough-talking macho man. They're anything but. The work fosters a deep regard for humility and careful talk. Living on the edge makes a person philosophical. Their era has passed and the new one is coming, but they aren't bitter, at least not the ones in Bella Coola. As one of them says to me as he sips his coffee: "If a faller could get through the first two years without getting killed, the odds would shift in his favour. There are many, many ways to die out there, and you had to learn each one of them. I broke a few bones, but nothing serious. You had to love the job or you couldn't do it."

A few days after arriving in Bella Coola, I called the local provincial conservation officer, James Zucchelli, to see if he had any suggestions about places other than Tweedsmuir Park where I might see bears; and, like most people in rural communities, he was helpful to an almost embarrassing degree. It was mid-September, in the midst of both hunting season and fishing season, but even though he was heavily overbooked at work and had a two-year-old at home and was enjoying a rare day off, he offered to drive me around and show me some bear habitat. Zucchelli, a fit-looking man in his thirties, was dressed in plain clothes and driving his own truck when he picked me up, explaining that it would have required too much paperwork to wear his uniform and take the government patrol vehicle. He has been stationed in Bella Coola for five years, and is responsible for single-handedly enforcing the wildlife laws between Tatla and Bella Bella, a block of wilderness bigger than Belgium.

"I thought it was a crazy place when I first got here," he says. "In January it's thirty below zero up on the mountains, and that cold, dense air sinks and accelerates and comes howling down the valley. The wind roars like a jet engine. Everything is colder and hotter and bigger and wilder. I grow basil the size of lettuce leaves. It's like nature on steroids. The trees are big and the bears are big. The people have a real pioneer mentality. It's a one-man district and it's impossible to get on top of the workload, but I love it here and I never want to leave."

As we're driving through the valley, I show him the road where I camped out when I first came here. He slows the truck and we bump down the trail towards the river. Before we climb out, he takes a cautious look around for bears, then I follow him down through the trees to the water. It looks different than I remember it. It's more open, with more second-growth alder and underbrush. There's an old firepit with some broken pieces of beer bottle. Maybe our memories have a tendency to idealize. Surveying the long stretch of river and gravelly shallows, Zucchelli says that once darkness falls, there will be four or five grizzlies working this stretch of water. They tend to take turns. You can determine the dominance of the bears by when they arrive. The bears with less status feed during the early evening. The big boars own the nighttime, and the lesser bears stay away from them. No bear wants to spend the remainder of the season limping around with a couple of big infected bite wounds on its neck and legs.

Zucchelli says that when he arrived, the government had cut back on hunting to the point that the bear population was nearing the saturation level. "In my opinion, we don't need a high population of bears. We need a healthy population of bears. At high density, bears and people cannot coexist without conflict. I had this one lady, a single mother growing her own produce. Two family units of grizzly bears had claimed her yard as their personal turf, and they were not only fighting her but each other for ownership. And that's typical. It's all about food. The big boars monopolize the best fishing spots along the river. So the sows with cubs and the juvenile bears end up in people's yards because they've been pushed out of the good habitat. These marginalized animals are stressed out. Can you blame them? They get beaten up by the boars if they go near the river, and they get yelled at and chased by dogs if they go in the yards. So now you have pissed-off, stressed-out bears, and I have to deal with them."

He has culvert traps and foot snares that capture a bear but don't injure it. Adolescent bears out on their own for the first season and sows with cubs are the ones that tend to end up in his traps. "The big boars seldom cause trouble. I've caught huge boars that were such good citizens nobody knew they were around. The adult males tend to stay away from people, but everything gets unstable when the populations get higher. The lesser bears—the old ones, the young ones and the females with cubs, and so on—are fighting to fit in. We had this crazy little grizzly up by Firvale that charged everybody. He charged cars on the highway in the middle of the daytime. A bear like that is not a good candidate for relocation because there's nowhere for him to go. He can't invade another bear's space, so he will come back to his home territory again and again. Bears like that usually have to be dispatched."

We keep driving, towards the Nuxalk First Nation, where we pull into the landfill, which also looks a little different from what I remember. There are no bears in sight and the place is quite neat, for a dump. A modest string of wire surrounds the perimeter. Zucchelli explains that it's a high-voltage electric fence, designed to keep the bears out. I tell him when I was here thirty years ago the dump was crawling with black bears. He says that changed when the grizzly population started recovering. By 2004 the grizzlies had taken over and the black bears were gone. These grizzlies rapidly became garbage-conditioned. He says it was the same dangerous situation that had been allowed to develop in other places. "We all got together and agreed the situation was unacceptable," says Zucchelli. "It was an accident waiting to happen. My orders were to clean it up."

Zucchelli spent a long time assessing the bear trails and looking at tracks and figuring out which bears were garbage-addicted. He says the provincial government, with the advice of bear biologists, has developed standards for determining which bears are addicts and which have a chance of rehabilitation. But in general, once a bear has the garbage habit, there's little hope for it. If the dump were to be closed off, the bears would just go looking for food in town. A bear with no fear of humans will even force its way into a building. "I studied them until I had identified twenty-one regulars," he says. "Everyone agreed they had to die because the First Nation is only two hundred metres away and the band council didn't want the spillover. We couldn't relocate most of them because they'd lost their ability to feed themselves. [He relocated two.] I didn't like destroying them. But a garbage-addicted bear is not the beautiful animal you think of when you say 'grizzly.' It's a sick, unhealthy animal with a cut-up tongue from eating tin cans, paws that are all infected from broken glass and a diaper hanging out of its ass. It has lost the ability to support itself."

After he hunted down and killed the garbage bears, the government fenced the dump, and now there's rarely a problem, although sometimes an innovative grizzly will try to get under the fence, lifting the wire with its shoulders and grimly absorbing the 7,000-volt charge. "They're such tough animals," he says. "One bear was shouldering the wire and letting the current burn his fur and skin. He'd just stand there, soaking it up. He was deliberately running down the solar batteries. He'd learned how to defeat the system and had scars all over his back to prove it. I put out a snare for him, and he charged me. I shot him, and he ran into the bush. They're not like black bears. When you hit them hard with a heavy rifle, they barely show it. The next morning I went into the bush to fetch him, and another big grizzly was there, eating him. And *he* charged me too."

He says the most dangerous animal in the woods is a grizzly bear guarding a food cache. The bear doesn't recognize the niceties of ownership. He doesn't care if it used to be yours; now it's his. As we drive up the valley, Zucchelli turns off at a sideroad and we head up Salloompt Road, winding our way uphill past open meadows and creeping around sharp curves overlooking the river canyon. "An old-timer named Jack Turner lives up the road here. Two years ago he was attacked by a grizzly in his front yard. They had claimed his fruit trees. We thought it was one grizzly but when I responded to the call in the middle of the night, there were four bears standing on the road. They wouldn't let me pass. I couldn't shoot because it was dark and I couldn't be sure of anchoring them. With all the emergency personnel showing up, the last thing we needed was wounded grizzlies in the area. I thought it was a sow and three grown-up cubs, but later on, we found it was four males. A pack of grizzlies! It's unheard of, but these male bears had banded together to guard their food source. They were real aggressive too. They chased some coho fishermen. Then they scared the hell out of some guy who happened past on a bicycle. Then they attacked Mr. Turner in his front yard."

Zucchelli parked in the driveway, and we made our way through a small grove of apple trees to a ramshackle little building. We scaled a rickety plank and ducked under the sagging trellises. Zucchelli knocked on the door and introduced me to Jack Turner, one of the valley's most storied pioneers, a threadbare elderly man with an unsmiling demeanour, a sort of clipped, parliamentary manner of speaking and a gleaming dome of pink skin across the crown of his head where a bear scalped him. We chatted for a few minutes, but not long enough, in my view, to do justice to such an interesting man, so later that night, I called Mr. Turner back and asked if I could come back sometime and talk to him at length. People at the hotel had cautioned me that he was a reclusive and difficult man, but he agreed to see me, "on one condition."

"And what is that, sir?"

"That you don't elaborate."

"Elaborate?"

"Writers tend to elaborate," he said. "I've spent a lifetime reading, and I know that writers make things up. So if you are going to write about me, then don't add fictitious details."

"Yes sir."

The next day I sat and talked to him in his little cabin, which was stuffed like a magpie's nest with books and curios, old bottles, ancient magazines and rows of strange rocks and minerals lined up along the windowsill. Baskets of green tomatoes and freshly picked apples were piled on the kitchen floor. A big wood stove with a crooked chimney wandered through the room before finding an exit in the roof. The room was heavy with the smell of woodsmoke and mouldy fruit. His old dog was arthritic, and there was a gangplank against the bed so the dog could climb up and down out of bed as it suited him. As we talked, the dog lay at Jack's feet, rousing occasionally to scratch passionately at some hard-to-reach flea. As Jack began his monologue, his legs were crossed and his hands were laced in his lap in the posture of a man giving a deposition. It was hard not to be distracted by his outfit—red long johns, an argyle sweater, a long canvas vest that was carefully stitched up with twine where the bear had ripped it open, pants that failed to cover his lower shins, unmatched socks, and chartreuse-striped New Balance sneakers. He didn't offer me coffee and he didn't ask why I had come. He merely sat in his chair and began his story in the businesslike manner of an individual who's been waiting a long time for this talk to take place. I didn't even have to ask him questions.

"I was born in Vancouver in 1931," he said. "It was a much nicer place then than it is now, but I didn't want to live in a city. I wanted to follow the outdoor life and to find someplace where I could live without being dependent on the cash economy. So in 1946 I left home with my Grade 8 in my pocket and started working at various jobs. I worked hard at logging and horse packing until I was in my twenties, saving money so I could get my own place. I wanted to get married, but I knew it would be hard to find a woman who wanted to live that way. In my spare time I travelled all of British Columbia and kept my eyes open. The only place I hadn't seen was Bella Coola, so I caught a mail train to Anahim Lake and walked over the precipice trail to Bella Coola.

It was the only way you could get in. Well, I stopped overnight at Atnarko, and there was an old bachelor living there and he asked me stay the night. During the evening while we passed the time, I told him about my plan and my hopes to find a woman who would share that life with me, and he said, 'Well, you should have been here yesterday. There was a young lady here about your age, and she wants to do the same thing.' He said she had gone to Vancouver to buy an airplane and learn to fly it. I thought, she sounds like my kind of person."

The young woman was Trudy Edwards. Her father was Ralph Edwards, the famous hermit of Lonesome Lake. Over the next two years, Jack Turner made several visits to Lonesome Lake, walking in on a difficult mountainous trail and getting to know Trudy and her parents. Trudy had built her own log house a couple of kilometres from her parents' home, and Jack volunteered to work for her for free. "After a period of time we decided we were compatible, and we were married in 1957. We had our first baby two years later."

They grew a garden and lived off the land. "We ate and lived very well," he said. "We grew tomatoes, pumpkins, squash, carrots, parsnips, radishes, lettuce, and bred our own fifty-day corn, similar to the type the Indians developed. It produces ears even in a bad year and has a nice nutty flavour."

They needed about ten sacks of potatoes but grew forty sacks in case of a crop failure. The surplus was stored in root cellars or fed to their livestock. They also raised cattle and horses. "It's impossible to raise pigs and sheep out there because the predators will take them. You stick to horses and cows because they can defend themselves—cattle with their horns, and horses, of course, are handy with their hooves. Horse meat is better than beef, but you have to trim off the fat."

They hunted deer for meat and never let an animal go to waste. "I had to kill a wolf that was bothering our animals. We made a saddle roast from it, but it had an unpleasant taste. Grizzly bear can taste fishy, but black bear is quite nice—even better than deer. Cougar and lynx have a white meat that tastes a lot like pork. I would never shoot a grizzly for food because the meat is poor. But I would sometimes have to dispose of a bear for defensive reasons, and we would always make use of the meat somehow."

Their homestead required about fifteen hundred dollars cash a year and about a thousand pounds' worth of store-bought supplies like flour, sugar, salt, lamp oil and gasoline for their little outboard motor. They made the hauling trip once a year. It was a long, difficult trail out to the road where the truck dropped their freight, and they would make several long lake crossings en route. "We would load the horses and supplies on rafts we built ourselves. You can determine how much a raft will carry by calculating the buoyancy of the logs. You measure a log's circumference and length, then you factor in the weight of a cubic foot of cedar, then you look at how high the log is floating in the lake. The horses went in the centre of the raft, and we pushed the whole works with our little kicker.

"We worked hard all day, every day," he said. "It was a good life, but most people wouldn't want to do it. People live in the city because it's easy."

They ordered books from the library and read in the evenings. "We didn't read trash," he says. "Our only interest was in works of literature. We read a book a week for forty years." A flock of endangered trumpeter swans lived on Lonesome Lake. The Canadian government paid them about fifteen hundred dollars a year to feed the birds in the hard days of winter, and that was their only income. Trudy's father had had an idea to buy a little Taylorcraft and use it to fly supplies in and out, which is why Trudy had acquired her pilot's licence. But her dad was bossy about who used the plane, and they ended up reverting to pack horses and carrying supplies on their backs.

The trail to Bella Coola traversed steep rock slides and heavily tangled swamps. With their string of horses, they would haul in tons of grain for the swans. "The horses carried wide loads, and you had to be careful they didn't push themselves off the cliff when they went around a tree. Every horse is a personality. Some can be trusted with responsibility and some cannot. We often met grizzlies along the trail. The horses were wary of bears and didn't like turning their backs on them."

In his careful and precise way of speaking, Jack explained that he generally got along well with the grizzlies and never shot one unless his life was in danger. "I don't believe in killing animals for pleasure," he said. "But of course we would all hunt for food. One morning in May I was going out to check on the cows, and I had a rifle slung on my back in case I saw a cougar. I came around a corner of the trail and an exceptionally large grizzly was walking towards me. He was perhaps a hundred yards away. As soon as he saw me he came at a run. They usually don't bother you, but evidently this one had gotten up on the wrong side of the bed. The gun was on a sling on my pack, and as I reached for it the sling caught on the pack. It took a second or two to free the strap. It was a Model 94 Winchester—which, as you know, is a lever action, so I had to work a shell into the chamber, which took another second or two. In one motion I levelled the gun and fired it at the bear's forehead. You never want to do that, because the bullet will glance off that thick skull, but

I had no choice because he was right there. Trudy heard the shot and she came. We measured with the axe and the bear had fallen dead three feet away. We skinned the bear and took the hide and the skull because there were always people who would be happy to buy these things. It was a very old bear, with blunt teeth, and the poor old fellow had a face full of infected porcupine quills, which explained why he was in such a foul mood. I sent the skull to a fellow in Vancouver and he dried it for a year, then had it officially measured, and it turned out to be the largest grizzly ever killed in North America. I sold the skull and the skin to a fellow in Corvallis, Oregon, for eight hundred dollars. He had it mounted, and it stood twelve feet high. A couple of years later, Clayton Mack, a local Nuxalk hunting guide, replaced it with an even bigger bear. He and his hunter found it dead in Rivers Inlet, but it counted anyway."

When Jack and Trudy got too old for the wilderness life, they moved into "town." He explained that they were both cantankerous individualists and got along better in separate houses. But he was obviously still fond of her. More than once he said, "You should be talking to Trudy. She's the interesting one."

In the fall of 2005 Trudy was away and Jack was taking care of her dogs. On October 19 he went out to feed her dogs, and his own old dog accompanied him. The dog ran around the corner of the yard barking, and then came running back with an expression on his face that said, "You take care of this." Four grizzlies were chasing him. The lead bear stopped and stood up when it saw Jack. "It looked about eight feet tall," he says. "So I went back in the house."

He gave the bears a few hours to go away. He still hadn't fed Trudy's dogs, so he left his own dog in the house so that it wouldn't repeat the performance and headed over to Trudy's home with a flashlight. He hadn't taken more than a few steps from the front gate when he heard heavy running steps. He turned the light in that direction and saw a big male grizzly coming. The bear hit him at a dead run and knocked him flying. "He grabbed my head in his jaws, shook me and pulled my scalp half off. Then he grabbed my arm and shook me the way a dog shakes a rat. Then he threw me into the bushes and walked away. It was all over in ninety seconds."

"Did you play dead?"

"In my opinion, all that advice they give you about whether to play dead or fight back is useless. When a bear attacks you it's like being hit by a train. You have no time to do anything. You're not even thinking. You're just being thrown all over the place."

"Why do you think he attacked you?"

"He didn't say."

Jack was silent for a moment. His old dog levered itself upright and rested its head on Jack's knee. He scratched it behind the ears and it dozed for a moment. If you adjusted for dog years, they were about the same age. "Most grizzlies won't bother you," he said. "I used to see them almost every day. But the odd one is aggressive. They're all individuals. You're always told to stay away from a mother with cubs, but once, I was crossing a log jam, and I got halfway across and abruptly realized a mother bear was on one side of me and two cubs were on the other. I was right between them. She watched me pass and didn't do a thing. Other times, I had bears come after me for no reason. It's very difficult to know what a grizzly is going to do."

After the attack, he crawled into the house. His arm was almost torn off and his scalp was down on his face like a mask. He was, he says, "bleeding very badly." He worked his scalp back up onto his head and settled it in place and tied it down with a towel. He tried to phone Trudy, but her phone was busy. His daughter's phone was busy too. He guessed correctly that they were talking to each other, and waited for half an hour for them to wrap up their conversation. He was thinking his old gal Trudy might be willing to drive him to the hospital. "I didn't want to make a big fuss and call an ambulance," he says, "but I began getting weaker and felt that I was going to pass out, so I called nine eleven. I told them I'd been attacked by a grizzly. They told me later that they thought it was a prank call because I was so calm. That's just my training from having spent a life in the woods."

Ten minutes later his yard was full of RCMP cruisers and emergency vehicles. He spent two weeks in a Vancouver hospital. The bites were infected* and he needed skin grafts. His arm was badly torn up and the nerves were permanently damaged. One ear was mostly gone, but he "still had enough to hang my glasses on."

There were photographs of him in the newspaper—close-ups showing a face and scalp that look as though they had been worked over with a chainsaw. Antibiotics saved him from the persistent infections that often result from bear bites. His caregivers

---

* Bear bites often become infected. In 1983 Canadian author Patricia van Tighem was hiking with her husband in Waterton Lakes National Park when they were attacked by a sow grizzly. Van Tighem was scalped, lost an eye and her face was permanently disfigured. Despite aggressive treatment with various antibiotics, she had many recurrences of infection. She was subjected to more than thirty reconstructive surgeries and had to endure the horrified glances of passersby. She wrote an international best-seller called *The Bear's Embrace*, but her post-traumatic stress was severe and ongoing. "There isn't a night I don't dream about it," she said. On December 14, 2005, she took her own life.

at the hospital urged him to talk to a psychiatrist, but he declined. "I'm fine," he says. "I've never had a problem with it. Not even a bad dream."

"Has it changed the way you live?"

"I don't go outside after dark," he says after a long moment of silent thought. "But that's not such an inconvenience. I usually spend the evening reading anyway. And if there are bears in the yard, well, it's a fair trade. I get the daytime and they get the nighttime. If you want to live in this country, you have to accept that bears have a right to live here too."

After we had talked for several hours, I noticed the afternoon was almost gone. The shadow of the mountain had filled his ivy-clad window, and it was getting gloomy enough that it seemed a logical time for him to stand up and light a lantern. But he didn't move, and nor did I, and the dog snored at his feet. I knew it was time to go, but he seemed accepting of my presence. It was one of those autumn afternoons in the mountains in which time seems to pause momentarily before you have to move on. I felt that I had spent many years talking with Jack Turner, even though I had only just met him. So there was a portentous silence that lasted for a few moments before I accepted the inevitable, screwed the cap back on my pen and closed the notebook. "Thank you," I said.

Out on his porch the evening was coming on, the mountains rising up towards a fading sky and a waxing moon. The air was sharp and cool. It felt like it might frost tonight. I shook his hand. "Maybe I'll see you next time I come through."

"Not likely," he said.*

---

* He died two months later.

After pulling out of Jack's driveway, I drove down the hill, stopping to get out and inspect the place where the four grizzlies came out of the bush and stood in the middle of the road, barring the passage of James Zucchelli's truck.

Down on the main highway, I rolled slowly past the field where Gary Shelton showed me my first grizzly two years before. It was a misty night, and I only recognized the spot because of the distinctive curve in the road. It was a good feeling to be getting to know this valley. I'd stopped frequently along this road in the daytime, checking out the bear trails that cross the road every mile or so like oversize rabbit tunnels through the underbrush. When I first arrived here, I never would have believed that those well-trampled paths were made by bears. Or that, now, these occasional heaps of dung on the highway were actually left by grizzlies.

Slowing the truck, I turned onto the little forest road that parallels Snootli Creek. As I bumped cautiously along the road, the headlights penetrated only a few yards into the fog. A miasma of spectral light hovered in front of the hood, vaguely illuminating the huge tree trunks and drooping ferns. I finally pulled to a stop in the clearing where Dave and I had pitched our tents so many years before. Cranking down the window a few inches, I breathed in the sharp aroma of deep forest, mould, rain and dying salmon. Opening the door of the truck, I walked to the edge of the woods and peed against a massive cedar. The tailpipe was muttering and I could hear faint music from inside the truck—a commercial jingle, the soft reassuring natter of civilization. Just a few steps beyond where I stood was the impenetrable darkness. The trail led to the river, where, as James Zucchelli explained, the big dominant grizzlies come to feed on salmon every night.

Even though I couldn't see the bears, I could feel their presence. The trees, the darkness, the soft falling rain—they all take on a spooky and alien quality when you're in bear country. All I would have to do is walk down through this clearing to the riverbank and I would almost certainly come face to face with a big wild male grizzly. Not many people can say they've done that. Would the bear ignore me or come at a flat run? It would be an excellent conclusion to my research.

I considered the possibilities for a few seconds, then climbed into the truck and drove back to the hotel to see what was on television.

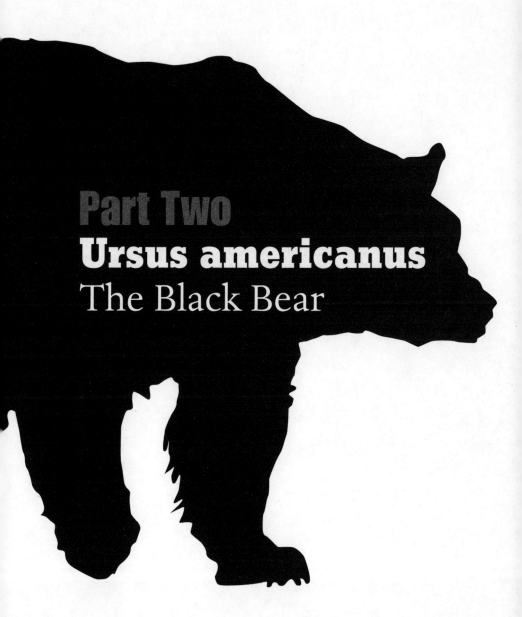

Part Two
Ursus americanus
The Black Bear

All the Bears
That Ever There Was

After the summer I spent looking for grizzly bears in the backwoods of British Columbia, I decided that I never again wanted to spend my summers working in a city.

The following spring, as university began to wrap up, I combed the newspapers looking for work in the remote reaches of Canada. Some friends of mine had heard that you could earn ridiculously good money working on the "green chain" at a northern British Columbia sawmill. It sounded pretty good, but when they arrived in northern B.C. and started their new jobs, they phoned me and said that under no circumstances should I ever, *ever* consider such a job. Then I heard a rumour that you could easily get a job in the Queen Charlotte Islands working as a "choker setter" on a logging operation. This seemed like a great idea, until I read Ken Kesey's novel *Sometimes a Great Notion* and learned that it is probably one of the hardest jobs in North America.

As always, coincidence intervened. As John Lennon once pointed out, life is what happens while we are busy making other plans. One warm night in May, I was playing shuffleboard and drinking beer at the local pub when some friends I knew from university told me they were all heading off the next day to work at a remote fly-in fishing lodge in northern Ontario. One of them had spotted the advertisement at the Manpower office, called the lodge owner, and he had hired all five of them over the phone. Now they were going to be "fishing guides." I didn't know much about working as a fishing guide, but it sounded a lot better than driving a forklift in a warehouse. I chiselled and pleaded with my friends until one of them agreed to call the lodge owner and see if he needed another guide. Twenty-four hours later, we were all jammed into a twin-engine Beechcraft float plane, cruising over the rumpled wilderness, heading for our new summer jobs at Bending Lake Lodge.

Guiding turned out to be my kind of job. You didn't have to worry about the mundane elements of daily life because your meals, laundry and dishwashing were done for you. It was like being twelve years old again. We spent our days cruising around in boats, getting a tan, catching fish and getting paid for it. There was nothing to buy, so we saved our money, and at the end of the summer I went home with a substantial little paycheque in my pocket. In many ways, it seemed like the perfect job. So the next year I applied for work at another lodge, and the following summer I went to work at yet another. The lakes were different, and the camps were many hundreds of miles apart, but in a sense they were all the same lodge. The culture of sport fishing was standardized. The American guests who came clomping down to the dock every morning with fishing rods and suitcase-sized tackle boxes looked like the same guys you'd fished with last summer, a thousand miles away, and in some cases they were. The boats were invariably sixteen-foot Lunds with twenty-horse Mercury motors. The shore lunch boxes contained the same stacks of plastic plates and magnum spatulas—wooden-gripped and long-handled so you wouldn't scorch your hands while working over the open fire. Fish were all rolled in flour and fried in lard the same way. Nobody knew why, exactly; there was just a doctrine, and if you departed from it or even tried to improve upon it in any way, you were only showing yourself to be some kind of subversive oddball trying to rock the boat. In every fly-in lodge in the north, the white guides smoked Sportsman cork-tips and the Indian guides smoked the harder-kicking Export A's. Guests were fondly remembered or bad-mouthed depending on how much they tipped. And no matter where you went, the woods were full of bears.

At Bending Lake there were bears on the path to the outhouse, bears peering from behind trees at shore lunch and bears prowling around the cabins late at night. These weren't grizzly bears. They were a different breed of cat altogether—*Ursus americanus,* the black bear. There are eight species of bears around the world, and since most of them have been exterminated from large parts of their former ranges, the black bear, with a population of about 750,000, has become the most abundant. Most of my fellow guides were Ojibwa Indians, droll raconteurs who appreciated this abundance of black bears for the element of chaos required for entertaining stories. There were always black bears on the island where we dropped our fish guts at the end of the day, and when anyone arrived by boat the bears would come galloping out of the bush, often provoking debate about whether they were keen on eating the fish guts or the delivery boys. One day, one of the younger native guides was dumping a pail of entrails when a bear came hot-footing it out of the bush towards him. He dropped everything and sprinted towards the boat, lodging a jam pail on his foot. The tale of him galumphing through the garbage with one foot clanging provided many chuckles at the dinner table that night.

Another day, two guides were ferrying loads of minnows across the lake. They carried the minnows in a large plastic garbage pail filled with water, and it was necessary to transfer them quickly to the big aerated tank alongside the lodge or they would die. When the guides arrived at the dock with a fresh load of minnows, they would lift the heavy pail out of the boat and hand it to two other guides, who would rush up the hill and dump it into the holding tank. The guys in the boat would then go and get another load. On their last trip, they were cruising across the lake with the empty garbage pail when they saw a bear swimming. It was a small bear, about the size of a dog, so they seized it by the scruff of the neck, dumped it in the garbage pail and clamped the lid shut. When they arrived back at camp, they handed the heavy garbage pail to their mates and told them to hurry, hurry because the minnows were dying. The guides rushed their burden up the hill, and when they removed the lid, out popped an angry bear.

At Bending Lake the native guides stayed in a large bunkhouse called the Swingin' Teepee. At the front of the bunkhouse was a spring-mounted door that opened inwards. One night, long after bedtime, a bear was nosing around the camp and smelled food inside the Teepee. Pushing through the door, the bear entered the cabin and began rummaging through the backpacks and lunch boxes. One of the guides, Pete Pronto, heard the odd snuffling noises, reached out in the darkness and felt something standing beside his bed. It was covered with fur. He shouted the alarm and scrambled out the window, followed closely by Stewart Kakeway, Thomas Paypompey Junior, Danny Pronto and about a dozen others. By now the bear was frightened and racing around inside the bunkhouse, woofing. It couldn't get out because the door opened inwards. The camp foreman, a grumpy, pipe-smoking woodsman the guides had named Shitty Smitty, was generally of the opinion that there weren't many bear problems that couldn't be solved with a high-powered rifle. He loaded his gun, stood at the window and fired one shot after another into the darkened interior, causing the bear to become even more frantic and bowl over the wood stove. The bunkhouse filled with smoke and might have burned to the ground, bear and all, if one of the kitchen girls hadn't noticed the faulty logic of the operation and propped the door open with a broom. At her suggestion, everyone retreated to the lodge and allowed the bear to leave the bunkhouse in peace. To urban sensibilities, these bear stories might seem cruel. But as far as the guides were concerned, the feelings of the bear were irrelevant. The only thing that mattered was whether the incident made good story material.

At Great Slave Lake, in the Northwest Territories, the bears were waiting when we arrived on the float plane to open up the camp in the spring. During the off-season, a bear had forced its way into the food storage building and made a fine mess. Imagine several hundred-pound sacks of flour emptied on the floor to ankle depth, combined with ten or twenty gallons of liquid bear shit, all of it mixed together and hardened to the consistency of epoxy cement. It took us a full day of hacking and scrubbing before it was possible to see the floor. On the second day, the camp manager was in the repair shop working on an outboard motor when a black bear appeared in the doorway and stood there eyeing him from twenty feet away. To say the bear was "eyeing" him suggests some kind of identifiable attitude on the part of the bear. But a bear's eyes reveal so little that he couldn't tell if it had come with intentions of friendly commerce or manslaughter. So he took a .300 Weatherby off the wall and racked in a shell. The boom of the gunshot rolled down the narrows of Great Slave, caromed off the cliffs and slopped back and forth for miles around like a shock wave in a bathtub, letting all God's creatures know that the humans were back in town. We heard the shot from the airstrip, where we were disposing of some rotting crates of decayed dynamite, and when we got back to the lodge, Ada Wilson, an Arkansas debutante who had signed on as a waitress and had never seen a bear before, was posing with the dead beast. After the unfortunate bear was immortalized in several photographs, we all went up to the lodge to eat. After dinner, someone went down the hill to skin the bear and observed that it was in fact gone. There was a big patch of blood on the shale, but the bear had disappeared. It had seemed very dead when we left it, but since it was too big for the seagulls to have carried off, we had to assume that it had gotten up and walked away.

That evening, our local version of Inspector Clouseau arrived, in the person of Louis Drybone, a diminutive sixty-year-old Chipewyan trapper who had spent most of his life in the wilderness. Louis barely spoke a word of English, but, with a mix of fractured phrases and hand signals he made it clear that he suspected the answer to the riddle. He began following an invisible trail across the hard ground and bare rock. Up the hill and into the forest he went, with the rest of us trooping along behind him. Louis had insisted on bringing a gun, which led us to assume that he thought the bear was still alive. But several hundred yards into the bush, he paused at a large, trampled-down clearing, which at first glance seemed to be the scene of a bear explosion. Bits and pieces of bear fur, shattered bone, ropes of intestine and pink connective tissue were scattered in every direction. At the centre of the clearing was a length of spinal column and a large lump of black fur with a front leg attached. The rest of the bear had obviously been eaten. Louis looked around the woods with a gleeful smile and said, "Barrens grizzly."

At the dinner table that evening, there was speculation that the photograph of Ada kneeling beside the dead bear might in fact show a grizzly off in the background, peering around the stack of oil drums with a glint of drool hanging from its chin. Ada sent the roll of film off to Yellowknife for developing. A month later, the developed film came back on board the camp float plane, which was piloted by Paul the pilot and our boss, Chummy Plummer. It was a calm evening and the lake was glassy. Paul misjudged his altitude as he was flaring in for the landing, and the old Norseman dug in its floats and somersaulted. The impact sounded like the world's biggest canoe paddle whacking the water. I happened to be down at the dock changing the spark plugs in my motor at the time, and after quickly tightening up the plugs was able to speed out to the crash site with another guide. By the time we got there, the front half of the plane had sunk. Ripped-up scraps of aluminum were floating in the lake, and amongst the debris, Paul the pilot and Chummy the boss were treading water. "Sorry to make you guys work overtime," the boss said as we pulled up. "Or maybe you just sped out here to rescue the beer." The film was lost with the airplane, and we never got to examine the photographs for a lurking grizzly.

During the summer, we had encounters with bears every couple of days. We saw an occasional wolf or caribou, but the black bear seemed to be the dominant life form in the sparse northern forest. There were bears and bears and bears. It was hard to imagine what they were eating—spruce needles? One day I was cruising in my boat with my guests along a desolate stretch of Great Slave when we spotted a bear making its way along a narrow talus beach at the base of a cliff. One of my guests grabbed his camera, so I headed towards the beach. At our approach the bear broke into a run. It couldn't climb the sheer wall, so it had no choice but to run down the beach. In short order, we'd caught up to it and were cruising along in parallel, taking pictures from a short distance as it galloped along the beach. Its ears were slicked back in fear and it was running full out, but when I lifted a trout from the fish box and waved it, the bear jammed its feet into the gravel and slid to a stop. It stood up, sniffed the wind and promptly belly-flopped into the water and swam towards us. Approaching the boat, it lifted a paw to find a grip on the gunwale. It would no doubt have climbed into the boat if I hadn't kept backing away. After marvelling at the bear's behaviour for a moment or two, we ended the game by throwing it the fish.

From this experience, one might guess that black bears are so obsessed with food that their hunger overrides any other drive, including panic. But every animal lives in its own world of phobias, and their mood swings may be no more explicable than ours. When we approached the lodge dump, some bears would run in terror; others would ignore us; others approach at a trot. Some black bears seem curious about people. At Great Slave Lake, the kitchen girls usually got a few hours off in the afternoon. The lake was too cold for swimming, but they would change into their bathing suits and soak up some sun on the shoreline. One day, Ada Wilson was down by the lake reading when she heard another of the girls walking up to join her. Ada kept reading. But after a while she thought it was curious that her friend had sat down behind her and not said anything. She looked over her shoulder and saw that in fact it was a large black bear, sitting so close she could have reached out and touched it. "I'm afraid of bears," she said. "But this one seemed nice. I just stood up and very calmly walked away. When I got up to my cabin, I looked down at the lake and it was gone."

This particular bear was a large and handsome male, and he became well known by the circumspect way he conducted himself. Almost everyone ran into him sooner or later, and all remarked on his behaviour. You had to assume he was looking for food, because that's a bear's main preoccupation every minute of the day, but why would he approach a woman and sit next to her? Narcisse, one of the Chipewyan guides, suspected the bear was his uncle Fred, who'd died recently. There were other theories, and they changed daily. The bear was like a guest star on an episodic television show. What was he going to do next? The bear seemed as peaceful as an old farm dog. And as soon as you saw him, you just understood there was no reason for fear. One day, for example, I was over at the airstrip, all alone, painting an overturned aluminum boat. It was up on sawhorses, and at one point, when I leaned over to load the brush, I felt a sudden twitch of that instinctive fear that sometimes shoots through one's nervous system when one is alone in the woods and catches an unexpected movement out of the corner of one's eye. As I peered under the boat, I saw a set of large, furry black legs sauntering past. "Oh," I thought. "It's just the bear."

I shared a cabin with two other guys, one of whom was Paul the pilot. Paul played the guitar and sang Marty Robbins songs and fancied himself to be a lone cowpoke born in the wrong era. Wilderness pilots are permitted to carry pistols for survival, so Paul had purchased a matched pair of single-action revolvers, which he kept in hand-tooled cowboy holsters slung over the foot of his bed. One was a .22 and one was a .44 Magnum. The idea behind the guns was that he would always be prepared for some dire emergency that would call for a cool nerve and lightning draw, but so far he'd only been provoked to the point of gunplay by empty oil cans.

One night, very late, we were all tucked into our beds asleep when I was awakened by creaking boards on the front steps and a tapping at the door. I assumed it was Paul's girlfriend, who often came to visit him in the wee hours. I called to him and informed him that his girlfriend was here. He got up and opened the door, then muttered some imprecation and reached for the holster hanging on the bedpost. A second later, there was a flash of light and an explosive bang as he fired the .44 through the screen door. There's nothing more certain to rouse you from a dopey sleep than the report of a big-bore revolver in a small room, followed by the bovine howl of a wounded bear. The bear turned out to be the big peaceful male everyone had become fond of, and Paul got a lot of grief from everyone, especially from the boss, who had to trek through the bush for several hundred yards in the middle of the night with a flashlight and a rifle and finish off the poor animal, whose lower jaw had been shot away. Why was the bear scratching at our screen door in the middle of the night? It couldn't have been attracted by tempting odours because we never stored food inside our cabin. Maybe it was curious about us for the same reason it was curious about Ada. It's hard to know why black bears do these things, because bears that reach out to people in a peaceful way don't tend to survive.

Close up, a bear's behaviour seems just as inscrutable as it is from a hundred feet away. At Great Slave Lake (or White Slave Lake, as the girls preferred to call it), bears often came to our noon-hour shore lunches. The smoke from the campfire would drift up into the woods, carrying the aroma of bacon and fish, and after twenty minutes one of the guests would spot a pair of black ears and a brown nose peering out from behind a bush. "Hey! Looka the bear." For the guides, it wasn't always fun to have a bear show up because we were responsible for making sure that everything went smoothly, and one could never be sure whether the bear would disrupt our work. Sometimes the bear minded its manners and sometimes it didn't. Some bears would stay in the woods until we left. Others would come closer, walking around the perimeter, trying to intimidate us with a display of half-lowered ears and a stiff-legged walk. One bear found some fish entrails and was wolfing them down when one of our guests slipped up behind it with a movie camera. As soon as he started the movie camera, the bear wheeled around and charged him. The young man dropped the camera, sprinted towards the water and plunged into the lake up to his chest. Pausing at the shoreline, the bear watched the young man thrash in the frigid water for a moment, then walked back to its meal.

Sometimes we had to pack up and leave because a bear was becoming too aggressive, trying to snatch food from the guests. At one lunch spot, a bear appropriated a boy's lunch and licked the plate clean. The boy's uncle decided he wasn't going to stand for this. "Back home on the farm, I've killed pigs bigger than that with nothing more than a sticking knife." He lashed a filleting knife to the end of a long spruce pole and advanced on the bear. The bear was still licking the plate and ignoring him. But when the man got within striking distance the bear deftly knocked the end off the makeshift spear with a quick swipe of the paw and burst after him. He ran down the hill with the bear on his heels and barked his shins as he leapt into the boat. Again, the bear could have caught him in two strides if it had wanted to, but it was only making a point.

Field studies undertaken by bear biologists suggest that a black bear will retreat if you stand your ground or stamp your feet and make a little counter-charge. But some bears don't seem to get the message. And anyway, few people are interested in running towards a bear to test a theory. Most campers and hikers would be satisfied to know whether a given bear is eyeing them with benign curiosity or malicious intent. When you encounter a prowling dog on a lonely road, you can tell by the dog's body language if it's going to behave in an aggressive way. With a bear, it's not so easy. Bears seem to have what psychologists call poor eye contact. They seem to be looking around you and past you, like the individual at the cocktail party who's not really interested in your banter.

A bear's irises and pupils are both black, so its eyes are as dark and indecipherable as the gaze of a B-movie zombie. Bears are so hard to read that people tend to fill in the blanks with their own preconceptions. Walking through the woods, nosing at a rotted stump, rubbing its rump against a rugged old tree, a bear is just a bear. But as soon as it encounters people, it becomes a symbol, a living inkblot that thrills one person and terrifies another.

How can we deduce a bear's intent? Park rangers, biologists and wildlife officers are always being asked what bears are "really like." Will a black bear stick its nose into my tent when I'm out camping? Will it run away if I bang some pots together? What should I do if I run into a bear on a hiking trail? Are they harmless? Are they dangerous?

A biologist, an animal behaviourist and a lifelong woodsman might offer three different perspectives on these questions, and all might even disagree, and all might be wrong. Who's to know? The bear knows, but he's not talking. In the few aboriginal societies that still maintain a close relationship to the land, the elders usually decline to offer any explanation of why a certain animal acts a certain way. An old Ojibwa guide named Junior Robinson once told me that he watched a bear taking a bath in a creek. "The bear was lying on his back blowing bubbles, and breaking them with his claw."

Junior shrugged as he told me this. He didn't try to draw any conclusions from the bear's behaviour. He just offered it as another piece of the puzzle. Perhaps if you gathered a hundred stories like that and shook them in a bag, you'd be left with some vague idea of what black bears will usually do under this or that circumstance. As Sherlock Holmes once put it: "You must first eliminate the impossible and whatever remains, however improbable, must be the truth."

Round Up the Usual Suspects

Kenora, Ontario (population 15,000), calls itself a city, but it's more of a small town, a picturesque resort community with a business district of four or five square blocks. Until a few years ago, the Trans-Canada Highway ran right through the middle of Kenora, and every car, motor home and semi-trailer crossing the country had to negotiate the main drag. Every day, hundreds of big transport trucks came wheezing and lurching down Main Street, bouncing up onto the sidewalk as the drivers cursed and cranked their way through the hard turn at the pharmacy.

Kenora is set firmly in the rocky terrain of the Canadian Shield, and even in the downtown business district there's a whiff of pine forest. From every street corner you can look down the hill to the Lake of the Woods, an immense body of water with more than fourteen thousand islands that sprawls across two Canadian provinces and the northern state of Minnesota. People in Kenora tend to get around by boat almost as much as they do by cars, and float planes are as common as taxis. In front of the Royal Bank, bush planes swoop in at rooftop altitude every few minutes, startling visitors with their teetering wings and growling engines. Nature here is growing up between cracks in the sidewalk. Vacant land and roadsides are covered with willow and other quick-growing species, and wooded shorelines provide travel corridors for skunks, foxes, coyotes and other wild animals that slip into town during the night. Black bears come and go, hitting dumpsters and garbage cans. "We even have bears living full time within the city limits," says Kenora resident Sarah Fairfield. "They have their hideaways in patches of bush. The mothers teach their cubs how to survive in town, and those lessons get passed on from generation to generation. Our urban bears know the good places to sleep, the places to avoid and the safe places to grab a free meal. They're like street people with fur coats."

Fairfield, a single mother with three kids, works as a bylaw enforcement officer for the City of Kenora, and her job is to ride herd on the local bears. In her uniform, she presents a nononsense demeanour as she leaves her office in the Kenora police station and walks out to her patrol truck. A stocky redhead prone to curt witticisms, she wants to make it clear that she doesn't so much have bear problems as people problems. "People do stupid things, and then they blame the bear. I had this one guy, for example, who claimed a bear tried to attack him. Well, then I recovered a video showing him feeding it M&Ms, which he sort of forgot to mention. Bears are very straightforward. It's the people who are hard to figure out."

Like a cop who always has to deal with the same group of quarrelsome drunks, she has a demeanour that vacillates between kindergarten-teacher patience and barely-contained anger. At an ice cream stand not far from her office, she answers her first complaint of the day. The owner has called her to demand that she remove a bear that has been breaking into his outbuilding. Parents with small kids sit on nearby benches, licking soft-ice-cream cones and watching the owner confront her. "It's a big bear and it comes almost every night," the businessman tells her in a heated voice. "I keep calling the city, but nobody does anything. I'd shoot it, but it's an urban area and the cops will give me a hard time. It's very frustrating. As far as I'm concerned, it's going to be your fault if this animal attacks one of my customers."

She nods evenly. The owner is a foot taller than her, and loud enough that you can hear him across the parking lot, but she stands with her thumbs hooked in her belt, looking unimpressed as he finishes his tirade. "Can we have a look at your outbuilding?" she says.

They walk across the parking lot to a storage shed on the edge of the woods. For the next five minutes she speaks to him quietly, pointing to various features of the doors, hinges and latch. He looks annoyed, but after a while he seems to nod in grudging agreement. Eventually, she walks back to the truck, and we head for the next call. "That's a fairly typical situation," she says. "The guy stores his garbage—in this case, pails of sour ice cream—in a shitty-ass little shed with flimsy plywood doors and he wonders why the bear keeps breaking into it. I told him, 'Listen, I am not interested in setting bear traps next to a shed full of attractants. I will set a trap in this case, but you *have* to fix your shed.' Because it'll only be a matter of days before another bear shows up. Many people in these backwoods towns have no patience with wild animals. A bear shows up on their property, right away they want to shoot it. Myself, I want to see legislation that empowers officers to write a ticket if you're mismanaging your garbage and attracting bears."

A few blocks away, she slows down as we pass an elementary school. Rolling down the window, she studies the crown of a tall poplar tree. "If you want to find bears in the daytime," she says, "look up. Bears like the coolness and the security of a tall tree. They'll pull the branches together and make a bed for themselves. There's often a sow bear sleeping in the top of that tree. It shows you how harmless these animals are. She's been living in town for years and she never bothers anyone. She sleeps in a tree next to a schoolyard and nobody knows she's there."

She says there are many bears like that, street-smart animals that know the rules and seldom get in trouble. "They use the same bush corridors and traditional trails. Some people live next to a bear trail and they don't realize it. There's one lady who phones in a complaint almost every day because she sees bears crossing her property. Well, madam, you bought a house on a bear trail. What do you expect? Over at Beaver Brae High School, there's a traditional bear trail through the bush right behind the school. The kids go out behind the school to roll joints and the bears walk by and they all get along fine. Kids nowadays are more respectful of nature than their parents. We give out Bear Wise pamphlets to the kids in the hope they'll read the materials and educate Mom and Dad."

We pull into the driveway of a small home with a shady backyard. Under a big apple tree at the head of the driveway is a trailer with a large steel box mounted on it—a bear trap. "This guy has apple trees in his yard, so the bears like to come through and clean up the fallen fruit. I think it's a little silly having fruit trees around here unless you like having bears in your yard. But you can't stop people from doing what they want on their own property. They call me up—'There's a bear in my yard! You have to come and trap it!' Well, sir, it's there because you attracted it."

Hauling a sack of bait out of the back of the truck, she inspects the trap. She says marshmallows, dog food, fruit and doughnuts are good baits. So is molasses. She says you don't want to use too much bait, just enough to get the bear's interest, and it has to be freshened regularly. "Everybody thinks that bears like rotten fish and so on, but they don't. They are fussy eaters, and if you don't change the bait every day or so, they won't touch it. They're also very smart. I've worked with dogs all my life, and bears are much more intelligent. A lot of bears won't go in a trap—they're suspicious. They'll stand up and push at a trap with their front paws, and if it's unstable they won't go inside. Once they get caught they're a lot harder to catch the next time. After a bear has been in a trap, you have to give the trap a good cleaning because the smell of fear remains and another bear won't go inside."

She says a lot of wildlife officers still use bear traps made from galvanized sections of culvert with heavy-gauge steel screening at the end, but she no longer uses them. "They're inhumane pieces of crap. The bears bite at the screening and break their teeth. We get these box traps custom made at Cambrian College for about five grand each, and they work a lot better. We have nine traps, and during the peak of the season, in late summer and early fall, all the traps are working twenty-four hours a day. Last year we trapped and removed forty-two bears. The year before, we caught eighty-two bears and relocated them. Can you imagine that? A small town like this with eighty-two bears in it? And that's just the ones we managed to catch. Sometimes if there's an immediate need, I'll tranquilize a bear with the dart gun. But you have to be careful because you can overdose the bear. And I won't dart a bear when it's high up a tree because it's liable to be injured by the fall."

She's not afraid to deal with bears in close-up situations. "They let you know if you're doing something that makes them uncomfortable," she says. "They look inexpressive, but they have a body language you learn to read. A black bear will turn its head a certain way or make a chopping sound with its teeth. It might even take a little run at you. That's a bluff charge, and it's a bear's way of saying, 'You're getting too close.'"

Six years ago, she spotted an advertisement for this job in the local newspaper and applied for it, even though, by her own admission, she knew "nothing whatsoever" about bears. There were hundreds of applicants, but she was chosen because the board was impressed by her self-confidence and her lifelong experience with animals. "I have always taken care of animals. Right now I have two horses, four dogs and two cats at home. One of my cats was tortured and mutilated by someone who cut off its feet and tail. I take some satisfaction knowing that animal will never be mistreated again. My parents founded the local humane society, and if there was ever some problem with a starving dog or an injured deer or something, the phone rang first in our house. I learned ethics from them at an early age, and I took part in some protests having to do with animal welfare. One time, we protested the shooting of dogs. Another time, a travelling huckster came through town with a wrestling bear. You'd pay a few dollars to manhandle this poor animal in the beer parlour. We stood outside the pub where this so-called entertainment was supposed to occur, and I think we generated some support among the public. Even some of the local rednecks backed us up."

Her busy season for bears goes from June to September, and the rest of the year she is busy fielding calls about barking dogs, mismanaged garbage and nuisance animals like skunks and raccoons. "We even get an occasional wolf." She rounds up stray or abandoned dogs and cats and keeps them in the local pound. If no one claims the animals or offers to adopt them, she has them destroyed. "That's a very hard part of this job," she says. "It causes a high burnout rate. People just can't take the cruelty of it. I'm taking care of all these lovely, affectionate animals, and it just breaks my heart destroying them."

Her bear traps are situated in odd places. One trap sits in the parking lot of the city's industrial garbage facility. As we approach the facility we can see hundreds of seagulls and ravens roiling above it like dirty smoke. Tractors and garbage trucks bumble in and out the entrance. Inside the compound, there's a mountain of garbage as high as a barn. Sometimes when the garbage trucks arrive, there's a bear sleeping on top of the mountain of refuse, lost in a sleepy reverie as it waits for another shipment of food to roll in. It's hard to imagine a bear stupid enough to swap all that free food in exchange for a handful of molasses-soaked goodies inside the bear trap, but you never know. As Sarah says, "You won't catch a bear if you don't set a trap."

Continuing on her rounds, she visits a trap at a service station next to a busy intersection—no luck—and another at a sports bar, where a group of young men are sitting out on the sundeck drinking pitchers of draft beer. As she parks her truck, I tell her that a few days ago I was here, enjoying the afternoon sun and having a steak sandwich, when I spotted a lump of black fur walking past the railings about four feet away. The bear walked to the highway, waited for the traffic to clear, then ran across the road and disappeared into someone's backyard. As I watched the bear, the guy at the next table told me he'd gone grocery shopping a few weeks before and stopped here for a draft on his way home. It was a hot day, so he parked his vehicle and left the front window open. When he came out, there was a large, furry rump protruding from the window of his vehicle. A bear had climbed into the front seat and was wolfing down green grapes, peanut butter, apple pies—a whole carful of groceries. He yelled and the bear gave him a mild look. He yelled again and the bear bailed out the window and waddled off.

Sarah Fairfield is not surprised. "I've heard every bear story in the book." She parks the truck next to the trap. A grandfatherly-looking fellow is peering into the trap, directing his wife in what sounds like Dutch to stand at the gaping entrance so he can photograph her. You can't help wondering if the local tourism bureau might plant these bear traps all over town as a way of proving to visitors they're no longer in Europe.

The Dutch fellow smiles as Sarah examines the trap and refreshes the bait. "How lucky you are to have bears!" he remarks. She ignores him. It annoys her when people approach her traps. When triggered, the trap door falls with an explosive bang that can easily take off someone's finger. She says that if that ever happened, they would blame it on her, not the person who ignored the warning signs all over the trap. As Sarah brusquely refreshes the trap she moves with a slight limp, the result of a riding accident she had a year ago. She was galloping on her horse, fell off and broke her legs. One of her feet was aimed the wrong way, so she twisted it back into place and stood up. "I'm used to taking care of myself," she says. "It didn't take all that long before the legs were healed and I was back at work. The bear traps are heavy, and even more so when you have a bear in them, so it's a physically demanding job. But I like the activity. I can't stand sitting around in an office."

If she catches a bear, she attaches the trailer to the back of the truck and hauls the animal about two hours north to a remote wilderness location. It has to be taken far enough that it might be discouraged from returning, which usually means a jaunt of at least fifty miles. "Some of them come back," she says. "Bears are homebodies by nature. But it's hard to tell which ones are returnees because they all look pretty similar. They tend to specialize in one particular way of earning a living, and they don't like to start all over again. A bear that specializes in freeloading at the Kentucky Fried Chicken outlet will cross hell and high water to get back. I had this one animal, Bear 240. I dropped him ninety kilometres away and saw him back at the Second Street bakery ten days later. Female bears are particularly committed to the specific territory they were raised in. The young males, well, they're like young males everywhere— they don't seem to have the same attachment to home."

Relocating bears is expensive. The entire procedure takes four and a half hours of her time, plus fuel and vehicle costs. She won't relocate a bear in the heat of the day—it's too hard on the animal—and she won't take anyone along and won't divulge where she releases them. "If I told anyone where I'm taking them, I guarantee there would be bear hunters there in camouflage outfits, waiting for me to let the bear out of the trap so they could shoot it and have it mounted with a snarl on its face."

Some animal control officers are careful about releasing trapped bears. I talked to one game warden who told me he backs the trap halfway into a shallow lake so that the bear must swim out. Climbing atop the trap, he draws his pistol, raises the door and scrambles back into the truck before the bear can swim up on shore and grab him. Sarah chuckles when I tell her this. "I park at the edge of the woods, get out of the truck and open the door of the trap. The bear walks out of the trap and gives me an inquisitive look. I say, 'Go on, get out of here.' The bear goes into the woods and that's the end of it."

She says that when people find out what she does for a living, they want to know if she's ever been attacked. "It's a bit silly," she says. "People have the wrong idea about bears. I carry no weapons, just a radio. I don't even carry pepper spray because I don't care to be sprayed in the face, which is a mandatory part of the training. I have removed literally hundreds of bears. I'm handling up to twenty complaints a day and I've never met an aggressive bear. People think bears are more dangerous than they really are. They're not scary at all. If I only had to deal with bears all day, my job would be a breeze."

* * * *

Sarah Fairfield's argument that people are the real cause of most "nuisance bear problems" is supported by research in other urban areas of North America. For the last twenty years, suburbs have been growing out into traditional wildlife habitat. In mountain states like Colorado, California, Nevada, Idaho and Washington, heavily wooded hillsides are covered with million-dollar homes. These exurban communities are subject to all kinds of natural hazards like wildfires, landslides and flash floods, and are occupied by homeowners who invariably argue that governments and insurance companies should protect them from risks they wouldn't face if they didn't live there in the first place. When a bear appears on someone's back deck at nine o'clock on a summer evening, frightening the children and sending the Lhasa Apso into a frenzy of yapping, the homeowner invariably calls the authorities, believing that a bear in the yard comprises a public emergency. Nowadays the cop or wildlife officer who responds to the call is more likely to take an approach similar to Sarah Fairfield's. Instead of rolling into the driveway with emergency lights flashing and shotgun in hand, he or she is likely to arrive with a skeptical attitude and what some people might regard as an impertinent question: What have you done to attract the bear?

Dog food, bird feeders, compost, greasy barbecues, full garbage bins—they all draw bears. And if homeowners think it's their right to keep whatever they like on their own property, fewer and fewer lawmakers are agreeing with them. In the Lake Tahoe area, where the dwindling population of black bears is protected by law, one research study determined that of sixty-two black bear deaths, every incident was traced back to human activity. In Virginia, it was determined that if food attractants were removed by homeowners, a bear would return only once or twice after it learned that the food source was gone. Many cities, like Los Angeles, have taken to fining property owners who persistently leave bear attractants on their property, making the argument that just one careless homeowner can create problems for an entire neighbourhood.

The theory is that once bears become hooked on human food, they lose their natural survival skills and become subject to all the risks associated with living close to cities. They get chased by dogs, hit by cars and shot by homeowners. If they get trapped and relocated, they can starve in their new wilderness location or be attacked by a dominant bear whose turf they have inadvertently invaded. There's an old saying that "a fed bear is a dead bear," and it speaks to the fact that there's no end to the trouble that seems to ensue once a bear learns to associate humans with food. And the very act of scavenging on garbage is detrimental to the bear's dignity and health. A study undertaken by the Bronx Zoo's Wildlife Conservation Society determined that urban bears are in poor physical condition compared to wild bears. When black bears spend less time searching for natural food, they quickly become fat and out of shape. According to Dr. Jon Beckmann, the biologist who conducted the Bronx Zoo study, urban bears are about a third heavier and about 30 per cent less active than normal bears. "They're hitting the dumpster and calling it a day," he says. "Black bears and people can live side by side in perfect harmony as long as bears don't become dependent on handouts and garbage."

Numerous polls and studies, including an annual report by the London-based *Economist,* argue that Canada is the most desirable place in the world to live, and Canada's most desirable city is Vancouver. (The cities of Melbourne, Vienna and Geneva were close runners-up, while Port Moresby, Algiers and Dhaka were given the honours for worst cities in the world.) In Vancouver, the north shore is the best part of the city. And the most desirable community on the north shore is West Vancouver. Spread out along a south-facing mountainside, surrounded by thick stands of hemlock and towering fir, much of West Vancouver sits on land that was covered by primeval rainforest only a generation ago. Nowadays, the lucky resident of West Vancouver can sit out on his terrace with a single malt on his knee, gazing at the sunset, the freighters heading out to sea, the suspended necklace of the Lions Gate bridge, and comfort himself with the knowledge that this splendid city—this very neighbourhood, in fact—has been acclaimed by smart people in places like London and New York to be the very *sine qua non* of twenty-first-century civilization. If you don't mind all the bears.

Twenty years ago, bears in West Vancouver were relatively uncommon. The city had to deal with perhaps four or five a year. Nowadays there might be four or five nuisance bears *per day*. Some of these calls undoubtedly arise from the same animal. As a bear travels, barking dogs and banging cookware document its movement through a neighbourhood. The phones light up in the local municipal office, and by the end of the day there might be a dozen "bear incidents" on the blotter. But there are also many more bears than before. The typical member of the public, depressed by the worldwide deterioration of forests, rivers, glaciers and other features of the environment, tends to assume that bears, too, must be a dwindling resource, hunted relentlessly for gall bladders, trophy rugs and other trivialities. But bear populations across North America (including black bears, grizzlies and polar bears) are in fact healthy, stable and probably higher than they have been for many years. Black bears in particular seem to prosper in places where suburbia integrates with the forest. Like raccoons, crows, gulls, deer and other opportunistic species, some black bears actually do better in a semi-developed environment. Marginalized and less-than-successful bears wouldn't be able to make a living if not for the freeloading opportunities presented by the suburbs.

Larry McHale works for the City of West Vancouver. Like Sarah Fairfield, he is in charge of policing the city's bears. He agrees that many "bear problems" are in fact caused by people, and says that much of the rise in nuisance bear complaints can be attributed to the incursion of people into traditional bear habitat. In West Vancouver, for example, mountain bikers and hikers use the near-wilderness as their playground. Outdoor enthusiasts of all ages hit the wooded trails every weekend, bringing along their unleashed dogs, stirring up wildlife and sometimes pushing animals towards more built-up areas. But he says that the increase in bear complaints is probably caused mainly by an increase in bears. "Many of our urban bears are subordinate animals that probably wouldn't make it in a wilderness situation. We get a lot of sub-adults and female bears with cubs—the sort of animals that get bullied by the big bears back in the woods. They can't get access to the berry patches, salmon streams and other high-value feeding areas out in the wilderness. The big, dominant bears monopolize these areas and they won't tolerate competitors. So the lesser bears don't have much choice. They can slowly deteriorate and die or they can come here and scrounge a living from dumpsters and such. In a place like West Vancouver, a bear can sneak through the yards and find a meal every day without worrying about getting challenged by any animal tougher than a golden retriever."

McHale, who is fifty-seven, has worked for the city for thirty years. The outdoor life keeps him lean and fit, and he wouldn't be out of place working as a stunt double for Steve McQueen. When he's not wrangling bears, he's fighting fires, scrambling up and down the local mountainsides with heavy hoses and pumps.

He keeps a backwoods retreat in Williams Lake, B.C., but says he doesn't really feel the need for regular vacations because he enjoys his work so much. "I'm lucky enough to get paid to do what I love." His office is decorated with his favourite bear photographs. One shows a bear sunbathing on someone's front deck. Another captures a house cat with its fur puffed out in anger, standing nose to nose with a large bear. "Some bears are afraid of cats," he says. "No one knows why. I've got a photograph around here of a house cat that chased a full-grown bear up a tree."

On a normal summer day, it's not long before McHale's phone rings and there's a bear complaint to deal with. Out in the parking lot, we climb into his big four-wheel-drive truck and cruise down along Marine Drive, past towering firs and the cobbled driveways of fabulous multi-million-dollar homes overlooking the Pacific. The woods are so dense here that a bear could bed down for the day in someone's backyard and not be noticed. Coyotes also live full time here, digging burrows in hillsides and eating whatever they can kill. Some go from yard to yard, hitting doggie bowls and looking for vulnerable pets. McHale says they sometimes find coyote dens surrounded by a litter of cat collars with bells and name tags.

West Vancouver is split longitudinally by a busy freeway called the Upper Levels Highway. The lower half of the mountain is heavily developed all the way down to the seashore. Above the highway, homes march ever higher into the forest and the mist that often covers the top half of the mountain. McHale explains that the Upper Levels Highway makes for a formidable wildlife barrier. Multiple lanes of cars and trucks sail along at high speed, and any black bear that wants to get across it had better lace up his track shoes. "We get bears killed on the Upper Levels fairly regularly," he says. "Once they get below the highway, it's very hard to push them back. And it would be a hazard for motorists if we tried to chase them across the highway and back up into the woods where they came from."

I tell him Sarah Fairfield is studying a new tactic for managing urban bears—harassment. Some wildlife officers are experimenting with aggressive dogs and guns that shoot noisy shells called bear bangers. McHale says that he already uses intimidation. "When we trap a bear we sometimes use a tactic called a 'hard release.' When we let them out of the trap, we yell and make a lot of noise and sometimes even shoot at them with paintballs. The idea is to scare the hell out of them. And it works. I've used a hard release on bears and never seen them again. And that's good, because they're just going to get in trouble in the city. We want them to get back to their natural habitat and stay there."

Some bears are not easy to intimidate. Down near the water, well below the Upper Levels Highway, there's a large shopping complex called the Park Royal Mall that is flanked by dense residential housing, high-rise apartment towers and busy thoroughfares. It's not the sort of place you'd expect to run into a black bear, but McHale got a complaint one afternoon that a bear had been spotted in the back lane behind the shopping centre. He pulled into the lane and, sure enough, a four-hundred-pound male black bear was standing next to a dumpster. There was a big tree alongside the lane. McHale gunned the truck towards the bear, jumped out and ran at the bear, yelling angrily, "Get up that tree!" The bear stood looking at him, stone-faced. McHale stopped. "Okay, don't get up that tree," he said, and retreated to his truck.

As McHale approaches the address where the complainant lives, he slows down and scans the neighbouring yards. When we arrive at the address, he parks the truck in the driveway and takes a good look around. He says that when he goes out on a call like this, the bears often leave when they hear him coming. "They know me," he says. "They hear the diesel rattle of my truck coming up the hill and they take off. I'm the sheriff they don't want to mess with."

The homeowner here reported that a bear was in her yard about half an hour ago. As we walk up her driveway, McHale, out of habit, pauses under a big spruce tree and gazes up into the tangled limbs. (As Sarah Fairfield remarked, "If you want to find a bear in the daytime, look up.") Sure enough, he spots a bear clinging to the trunk of the tree about ten feet above his head. "A sow and two cubs," he announces.

I go to the base of the tree and look up at the bear. As is typical of mother bears, she has positioned herself between us and her cubs—two cowering furballs the size of raccoons. As I make eye contact with the sow, she hisses and pops her jaws, an urgent, hollow sound like a knuckle rapping on hardwood. McHale touches my sleeve. "Don't get too close," he says. "She might drop out of the tree and come for you. They're as fast as lightning, and the first time it happens it scares the hell out of you. It's just a bluff, and if you stand your ground she'll turn around and scramble back up the tree. But still, I've been charged seven or eight times and it's not a pleasant experience."

McHale walks up to the house and rings the doorbell. A woman of about forty comes to the door with two little girls, one in each hand. She tells McHale that the bears walked through the yard and climbed the tree when her tiny dog went insane. "Will they attack us?" she asks.

"No, they won't attack you."

She says, "Can we pat them?"

"No you can't pat them. Just stay away from them. They'll sleep in the tree all day. At sundown they'll climb down and go on their way."

He gives her some brochures and tells her to call him if there is any further trouble. As we pull out of the driveway and cruise down the street, a contractor driving the opposite way in a truck waves him down. "Are you going to trap those bears or tranquilize them or what?"

"They're not causing any trouble. We'll just monitor them."

"My men are trying to do a job here. It's not safe."

"The bears won't bother you."

"How do you know?"

"Just give her some space and she'll mind her own business."

The contractor is getting annoyed. He's in no mood for this sort of back talk from a city employee. "Listen, pal, you have to get those bears out of here."

"Sir, they're my responsibility, and I'll make that call."

"Yes, and it's going to be your responsibility if they attack somebody."

McHale says, "You can always call me if they come near your work site." He offers the contractor a Bear Wise brochure and his business card, but the man accelerates away.

McHale is silent for a few moments as we drive down the hill. He's obviously vexed. "That part of the job I don't enjoy," he says. "People come up here in the woods to build houses, and they expect the wild animals that have been living here for thousands of years to just go away. I think that if you choose to live close to nature, then you should try and learn a bit about wildlife. Those bears aren't threatening anyone. They're just trying to make a living like everyone else."

He says some people enjoy having the bears around—for instance, Penny and Nick Geer, a couple who live in a wooded enclave above the Upper Levels Highway.

The next day I talk to Penny, who tells me they're accustomed to seeing coyotes and bears in their neighbourhood. "There's a creek nearby and it's sort of a travel corridor for wildlife. Nick and I go for walks up on the mountain, and we usually wear bells because you often see bears along the way. I think it's wonderful to see them, but not everyone agrees with me. My eighty-six-year-old mother says, 'I won't be coming to see you if there's a bear waiting for me in the driveway.'"

One particular bear often showed up in their yard with its cub. "It was a regular visitor," says Penny. "She was a fine-looking bear with a thick, glossy coat. She'd come into the garden and graze on the grass and we'd watch her for hours. One morning Nick went down the driveway to get the mail and left the door open because it was such a lovely morning. When he came back inside, he heard a crash inside the house and he shouted, 'Are you all right?' Well, I walked out of the bedroom, and there was the bear right in the kitchen. She was about three feet away from me, and the cub was in the pantry. The mother bear stood up and peered into the kitchen sink to see if there was anything good to eat in there, and then she dropped back onto all fours and walked around into the dining room. She was totally relaxed. I clapped my hands at her and shouted, 'Out you go! I am not Goldilocks!'"

Penny says the frightened cub ran out the front door, which was still open, and the mother waddled after it. "'Out you go!' I shouted. She was very calm, and she kept giving us this look like, 'Do I really have to go?' When she was halfway out the door,

Nick gave her a slap on the bottom with the door to send her on her way. When it was all over, the reality of what had happened sank in, and our hearts started beating. After all, she's a wild animal and we're well aware how strong bears are. We've seen them take a steel post with a bird feeder on top and bend it over like a bobby pin just to get some sunflower seeds. But when I look back on it, there was no need for us to be frightened, because she was a placid, lovely animal and was never the least bit aggressive towards us. I have to say that when she stopped coming to the yard we were very sad."

One of Larry McHale's most interesting cases involved Peter and Lynn Henricsson, who live up in the nosebleed section of West Vancouver, so high that even your automobile sags with exhaustion as you climb the steep hill to their address. Their new home has an aviator's view of the ocean and of the hazy complexity of the city far below. Peter, a tall, slender, middle-aged man with that wholesome, outdoorsy look that seems to be part of the Scandinavian birthright, takes me out onto the rear balcony and explains that he was sitting out here one evening, enjoying a glass of wine with Lynn, when a bear walked into their backyard. "We weren't alarmed because we've seen lots of bears here," he says. "One time we actually had eight bears in our yard. This time it was just a little cub of about twenty pounds."

Peter went to get his movie camera, and for the next twenty minutes, he says, the little bear "treated us to the most wonderful display of animal behaviour. We had some tomato plants in the backyard, and he went from plant to plant, eating the tomatoes, sitting on his rump and tenderly holding each tomato in his hands and examining it before he ate it. The next day, he came back and spent a long time playing with a cedar plank in the yard. We were worried about him because he was so small and we couldn't see his mother, so we called Larry McHale, who came up and looked at it and confirmed that it was an orphaned cub."

McHale told them it was hard to know what had happened to its mother. If female bears go into hibernation in healthy physical shape, they sometimes have three cubs, but if the pickings are lean the following summer the third cub may be stunted and weak and will have a hard time keeping up with the family. He told them cubs on their own don't have much chance to survive. But for the rest of the summer the cub not only thrived but kept coming back to the Henricssons' yard. "We started calling him Beari," says Peter. "He didn't seem to be looking for food as much as company. He would stretch out in the sun on the deck right outside the glass door and just hang out all morning. He liked it best when we came outside and joined him. He was always playing with something or trying to get us to play with him. He clearly wanted to socialize."

Lynn says she has been frightened of bears all her life, and Beari probably sensed her nervousness. "He more or less ignored me and bonded with Peter. He treated Peter like his mother. He would suck on Peter's leather shoe for hours or climb up into his lap and suck on his thumb."

When autumn approached, Peter became worried that the cub didn't know how to hibernate and wouldn't stand a chance of surviving the winter. As Larry McHale recalls, "Peter called me and told me he wanted to find the cub a good home for the winter, and price was no object."

McHale said he couldn't help him. Black bears are so abundant that no one is much interested in feeding and housing strays. For one thing, it gets expensive to feed them, and they live a long time in captivity. When Peter found out there was no agency willing to look after Beari, he decided he was going to get some plywood and straw and build a hibernation den for the bear in his garage. McHale couldn't believe it. "I said, 'Listen, you can't do that. It's not only against the law but it violates every principle of wildlife management. This is a wild animal, and you have to let nature take its course.'"

Peter still felt responsible for the bear's well-being and continued to research possibilities. He phoned different animal welfare agencies. It's not legal to feed, capture or keep wild animals as pets without a licence, but he wasn't afraid of going the illegal route. "I found people who were willing to pitch in and help with Beari," he says. "We talked to this one animal shelter that offered to help us relocate him. We were going to use fruit/nut bars to lure him into a big dog kennel, then a truck would come in the middle of the night and we'd spirit him away, like in the days of the Underground Railway. We were ready to put the plan into action when Beari just disappeared."

Autumn turned to winter, and the Henricssons assumed that Beari had died or starved to death, or perhaps had been hit by a car or killed by a larger bear. They were sad, but there was nothing they could do about it. The next summer, Peter was sitting out in the yard when a large bear walked into the yard. "We see a lot of bears, but this one was so forward in the way it approached, I have to admit I was a little startled." It walked up the steps and started sucking his thumb. It was Beari.

Peter was overjoyed to see the bear, but it was much larger now. Lynn says, "We would come home and he would be sitting in the doorway waiting for us. He wasn't allowed to come in the house, so he would stand in the doorway and block us. And if we tried to get past him he would 'message bite' us. We did a lot of research on bears and we learned that this is how bears communicate. They give you nips or they swat you with a paw. The problem is these animals are unbelievably powerful. A bear can suspend its whole weight from one claw, so one swat with its paw or one message bite can really hurt you. It was getting to the point where he wasn't so cute anymore, and we realized we had to do something."

They examined his droppings to see what he'd been eating. Remarkably, the bear had been subsisting on wild food. "This made him a good candidate for relocation," says Peter. "So we talked to Larry McHale and made a plan."

One day when Beari was in the yard, Peter called McHale. A short time later, McHale and a provincial conservation officer pulled into the driveway and backed a mobile bear trap up to the garage. "I was worried when I saw the game warden," says Peter. "He was wearing a flak jacket and a uniform and looked very serious. He had a gun on his belt and he kept putting his hand on it as if he thought Beari might be dangerous. I was getting nervous about this man's attitude, but Larry said, 'Don't worry, he's a good guy.' I went into the garage where Beari was, and the conservation officer put his hand on his gun and said, 'Don't go in there!' I just ignored him and went into the garage and knelt down beside the open door of the trap and called Beari."

The bear approached Peter, peered at the bait and gave Peter a dubious look. "Beari didn't want to go in the trap," says Peter. "He was nervous. I patted him and told him, 'It's okay, you can go inside.' He went halfway into the trap, then backed out and sucked on my thumb for a while. He seemed to know that this was the end of our relationship. Sucking my thumb was his way of saying goodbye."

The bear went into the trap, the door banged shut and Peter burst into tears. "I had betrayed him," he says. "But at the same time I knew it was for the best. I was essentially his mother. I was not only his surrogate mother but also his mother because I sent him away for his own good, as mothers must do. I even felt proud of him. He knew how to open doors. I wanted to make a hibernation den for him, but he figured it out all by himself. He was such a smart bear."

Larry McHale took the bear far up the valley of the Fraser River and released him in what he describes as "an ideal wild setting for a young bear." Larry says that even though he had an official role in the matter, he developed a soft spot for the bear. "That was definitely the cutest bear cub I've ever seen," says McHale. "It was very friendly and full of mischief." Larry didn't tell Peter where he released the bear, thinking that it was better to make a clean break. He thought Peter might go looking for the bear, and Peter says he was right.

Peter says his association with the young bear enhanced his love of nature. "I feel I understand these animals so much better than I did before. Most of us fear bears because we think they're a threat to us. But the fact is we're a much bigger threat to the bears than they are to us. We're not part of their natural food, so we have nothing to fear from them. And I enjoy seeing them. The enjoyment we've derived from watching bears in the yard far outweighs any inconvenience or any damage they have done to our garden."

Lynn says that she, too, now has a different attitude about bears. "I've talked to experts and read lots of books, and the more I've learned, the less scary they seem. One day, we had this three-hundred-pound bear in the yard eating grass. She would slither along on her belly like a snake, eating grass as she went, looking as if she couldn't be bothered standing up. If you didn't know anything about bears you might think it was bizarre behaviour, but now I understand she was just trying to conserve every calorie of energy so she could put on more weight for hibernation. When you learn about them, you come to understand their reasons for doing things. I can honestly say I'm not as frightened of them as I used to be. I guess you could say I've been educated."

The Man Who
Talks to Bears

In all his years of dealing with black bears, Dr. Lynn Rogers says he has been injured "only" twice. Once, a mildly annoyed bear swatted him on the arm when he kept interrupting it while it was eating. Another time, he was visiting a high school class with a bear, and when the animal decided to leave the room, he unwisely tried to stop it. He says he's had a few Hail Mary moments, though. Once, an immense male bear walked up to him and closed its jaws on the top of his head. One false move and the bear would have bitten into his head like an apple. Was he worried? "Bears have their own language," he explains. "This big fella had told me that he wanted to be my friend. Now, I had never seen a bear do that before, so when he took my head in his mouth I thought, 'Oh, oh . . . is this that one bad actor of a bear that's finally going to do me in?' But I trusted him. He'd said he wanted to be my friend, and he wasn't lying. In my experience, bears don't lie."

Rogers is arguably the world's foremost expert on black bears. Most of the world's big, charismatic animals have their Boswells in the scientific community, whose names you encounter repeatedly when you read about the animals. Timber wolves have David Mech; grizzly bears have Chuck Jonkel of the Border Grizzly Project; polar bears have Ian Stirling; and black bears have Rogers, who is sometimes described as "the Jane Goodall of black bears."

Lynn Rogers has spent much of his life studying black bears, and they're pretty much all he wants to talk about. He has travelled with black bears, crawled into their dens, eaten their natural foods, collected their droppings, hauled their squalling cubs down out of trees and weighed and measured them right in front of their mothers, placed radio collars around the necks of wild adult bears without using tranquilizers, and, after a long day of tracking bears, observing their every move and making notes on his laptop computer, he has unrolled his sleeping bag at eleven or twelve o'clock at night and curled up beside them to catch a few hours' sleep.

For all his tireless study of bears, he is uncomfortable with being studied himself. He is relaxed with bears but wary of journalists, who in his view are less interested in balanced, accurate stories about bears than in stories that quicken the pulse—tales about bears in the schoolyard, bears breaking into homes in the middle of the night and, if you can find them, stories about wild-eyed bears ripping apart screaming hikers. He probably deals with most journalists the same way he deals with me, by ignoring their emails and screening his calls. When I finally catch him with the old tactic of dialling from a payphone, he confesses that he's not much interested in being interviewed. Yes, he's in the business of educating the public, and yes, he wants people to learn the truth about black bears, but he'd rather take his message straight to the people without a detour through the halls of journalism. Even when I tell him I'm interested in both sides of the story, he doesn't seem impressed. "I don't think the story has two sides."

So our phone conversations tend to consist of him trying to wrap up the call and me trying to keep him on the phone. Despite all that, Rogers is a pleasant fellow and he seems to have that small-town reluctance to give offence. After several calls, he finally agrees to meet with me if I come out to Minnesota for a visit. His turf is the small town of Ely, which is located in northern Minnesota, in the Superior National Forest, a swath of wilderness that was set aside for permanent protection by the original Teddy Bear, Teddy Roosevelt, in 1909, and is still the largest chunk of wilderness in the eastern United States. If you cross the border from Canada and drive south along the shore of Lake Superior, you travel on a highway that is wide and empty, with the vast blue-pastel plane of Gitche Gumee looming into view every time you top a hill. The mountains here are ancient, so old that they have been worn down to blunt humps. There are not many people in this part of the United States and, not coincidentally, lots of wildlife. The woods are full of deer and moose, and all those herbivores support a population of about four hundred wolves—the largest in the lower forty-eight states. On this summer day, the long stretch of winding two-lane to Ely is utterly deserted, with deer popping out of the woods every few miles. In more than an hour of driving, only one vehicle passes me, an SUV wearing the star of the Minnesota State Patrol, its high undercarriage and rugged tires testifying to the fact that summers around here are short.

Ely is a small town but is prosperous because of its proximity to the Superior National Forest and the Boundary Waters Canoe Area. Every summer, the town fills up with campers and canoeists, and its main street is dedicated to stores that rent canoes and sell camping gear to tourists. A few miles outside Ely, a gravel road leads through the woods to Lynn Rogers' rustic home. It's a two-storey house with a big stairway leading up the side. His living quarters are on the second floor, and as I mount the stairs I can't help notice that a large black bear and two small cubs are on their way down the stairs toward me. I stop and wait to see what the bears are going to do. But the mother bear has also noticed me and has reversed her steps up to the deck, where she stands waiting for me to come up. For a few moments we stand there staring at each other, caught in a politeness contest. After waiting a few seconds the bear relents and comes down the stairs and leads her youngsters into the woods. At the top of the stairs I knock on the door. A tall, sandy-haired man in his sixties answers the door. He looks like a logger, with workboots, blue jeans and a checked flannel shirt. From inside the kitchen comes the aroma of chili and garlic toast. He and his researcher, Sue Mansfield, are making dinner and they've been holding off for my arrival.

Like a lot of men who work in the woods, Rogers seems to have somehow avoided growing up. As he prepares dinner, he moves around the kitchen with the nervous energy of an adolescent, and he seems excited about the fact that my arrival means he can finally sit down and eat. He also seems more relaxed about being profiled, which might be due to the fact that I'm on his turf and he's accustomed to re-educating people about bears. While Sue dishes out the chili, I tell him about the bears I just met on his stairway.

"Okay . . . so you met the bears," he chuckles, rocking up and down on his heels like a schoolboy caught with a slingshot. "Well, bears are regular guests at this place."

Every summer, he holds workshops for people who want to learn more about bears. His home is incorporated under the name of "The Wildlife Research Institute," and it has enough room for eight guests. Over the course of three days, he and Sue teach the workshop participants about bear vocalizations, body language, social organization, diet and other aspects of bear society. They show the students film clips and play audio tapes of bears communicating. "We get people from all across North America," he says. "Wildlife professionals, naturalists, outdoor recreation buffs and, really, anyone who enjoys wildlife. But the program is very helpful for people who are afraid of bears. We get lots of folks who say they would really enjoy going camping or hiking in the summertime, but they are too frightened of running into a bear. That's very sad, but it's quite common. I don't know how many times I've talked to people whose first question is 'How dangerous are bears?' I tell them to relax, because their fear is based on misinformation. For many years the magazines, television and Hollywood have been spreading all kinds of nonsense about bears."

Sue Mansfield has been working with Rogers since 2001. An expert in tracking and animal behaviour, she takes the students on walks through the forest near the Wildlife Research Institute and shows them the subtle signs that wild animals leave behind.

Mansfield also knows the kinship relations among the fifty-odd bears in the study area and knows each bear's individual personality. She can say which young bears are the offspring of which adults; where those young bears have dispersed to; and whether they have managed to produce their own families. She and Rogers have put radio collars on about a dozen bears, and they study the activity and behaviour of those animals on a long-term basis. They also know a number of wild bears that have learned to trust them, and they frequently follow these animals at close range to gather data about their feeding habits. In addition to these outings, the students are exposed to the bears that constantly come and go from the feeding station on the upper deck. "On a busy summer night we'll have up to eighteen bears visiting the deck right outside the window," Roger says.

"I've always been told that it's wrong to feed bears."

"People feed hummingbirds and chickadees—why not bears? I've been feeding them for years, and there's never been a problem."

"Doesn't it teach them to associate humans with food?"

"No, it teaches them to associate Lynn Rogers with food."

"But game wardens say that most of their problems with nuisance bears are caused by bears becoming addicted to human food."

He shrugs. "I happen to think that most of the conventional wisdom on bears is wrong."

Rogers says he shaped his opinions over forty years of life in the north woods. He grew up in rural Michigan and always loved animals and the outdoors. As a young man, he worked as a postal carrier and always had a pack of dogs following him on his rounds. Sometimes the small ones would hitch a ride in his mail sack. In college, he studied biology and took an interest in wildlife, especially bears. In those days, black bears were considered vermin; they had no protection under the law and could be shot without a licence year round. The more time Rogers spent in the woods, studying bears, the more he realized that people were wrong about them. They weren't stupid, lazy and potentially dangerous—they were mild-mannered animals that showed intelligence in everything they did.

One of his first accomplishments was to get bears listed as game animals in Minnesota, which meant there was a regular hunting season and a licence was required to shoot one. It also meant that state biologists could keep an eye on their population and curtail the hunt if numbers were getting low. Counter to what you might expect, he's in favour of sport hunting for black bears. "I always ask myself, 'What's good for the bears?'" he explains. "Sow bears will always overproduce cubs. But there's a limited carrying capacity to the habitat. It's the same with all animals— a given habitat will only support a certain number of a given species. So you often end up with more bears than the area will support. In a wilderness scenario, those bears will die of starvation or get injured by larger bears. In a more developed area, they will get in trouble with landowners, and many will get shot as 'nuisance bears.' So a certain number of surplus bears are going to undergo a miserable death every year no matter what. From a humane point of view, I would rather see a standing bear at a bait station get shot and killed cleanly, at close range, by a trained hunter than to see it wounded in the middle of the night by some frightened homeowner who botches the job and leaves the bear to run off and die in misery. In other words, it's not about whether hunting bears over bait is sporting. It's about whether it's the most humane way to control the population."

Black bears tend to live out their entire lives in a defined area. Growing up, a young black bear will become familiar with every rock and tree in its home range. When its mother ejects it from the den, it will be allowed to stay in the general neighbourhood for the remainder of its second summer. But by the following year it will be shooed off to find its own territory. A sow will usually tolerate the proximity of her daughters—they might set up a home territory of about five square miles adjacent to their mother's—but her sons must travel long distances and find a home turf of about fifteen square miles they can occupy and defend. This is not easy. A bear can't simply show up one day and start living in a piece of woods any more than a young man could decide of his own initiative to pitch a tent in Tony Soprano's backyard. Older males will not tolerate the presence of sub-adult males—large boars will even attack and kill their own male offspring—so it's not easy for the juvenile male bears, and these are the ones that tend to raid campgrounds and cottages.

By feeding local bears, Rogers may actually be helping them to stay out of trouble elsewhere. As we're talking, a heavy creaking on the outer stairs announces the arrival of another bear. This one feeds for only a minute, then leaps up onto the railing and tiptoes along the top of it like a tightrope walker. It's a good twenty-foot drop to the ground, but the bear doesn't seem concerned about heights. Everyone is silent as we watch the bear leap down off the railing and amble past the front entrance, which is open except for the screen door. This is what his students do in the evening: sit here and drink their after-dinner coffees and watch the bears. Having gulped down a few mouthfuls of food, the bear once again leaps up onto the railing and takes a daredevil stroll around the perimeter. It's a fascinating display of agility and nonchalant ursine behaviour, but not everyone would find it enjoyable. If the average backwoods landowner looked out the window and saw a bear walking around on his deck, he might rush to the closet to get his rifle. Rogers tells me one local guy boasts that the best thing to do with a trespassing bear is shoot it in the belly with a .22 so it dies of peritonitis, days later and many miles away, and you don't have to dispose of the body. I know an old-timer in the backwoods of Ontario who told me he usually kills a bear as soon as it comes into his yard, on the grounds that it's a cocky bear that he'll sooner or later have to shoot anyway.

I know another fellow who has had his cottage broken into twice over the last couple of years. He phoned the Ministry of Natural Resources, and they weren't much interested, explaining that they get these calls every day and no longer have the budget to remove nuisance bears. He phoned the Ontario Provincial Police, and they weren't much help either, but they asked him if he owned an adequate gun. He answered yes. The cop told him he was enti-tled to shoot the bear as long as he disposed of the body afterwards. So that's what he did. The second time he was home-invaded, the bear clawed a hole in his veranda wall, moved into his cottage and lived there for the better part of a week. It tore the door off the fridge, ripped the lid off the chest freezer, and sent a good hundred pounds of thawed lamb, shrimp and sausage down its alimentary canal and out its rectum, using the heirloom carpet in the living room as a dumper. The damage amounted to over ten thousand dollars, none of it insured, the bear being an act of God. Accus-tomed to hearing these stories, I'm a little surprised that Rogers can get away with this—not legally, but in terms of encouraging the bears to believe they have the run of his property. "Don't they ever try to come in the house when you're not here?"

"Why would they do that? The food is outside."

"What about in the middle of the night, when it's quiet? I mean, the fridge is full of good stuff. You're cooking chili and garlic toast. There are all these delicious smells in the house. What self-respecting bear wouldn't at least try to rip off the front door when you're asleep?"

"They know the rules."

"What do the neighbours think?"

He shrugs grandly. "Let's ask one." He flips open the phone book and searches a number. "This fellow lives about five hundred feet away. You can ask him if he's ever had any trouble with these bears."

He hands me the phone, and I talk to the gentleman, explaining why I'm here. The neighbour says he doesn't have strong opinions about bears one way or another but says that in five years he's seen only one bear on his property. "That was probably my fault because I left a bag of ripe garbage in my garage."

"Does it bother you having so many bears right next door?"

"I never see them."

After I hang up, Rogers says the bear feeder on his deck illustrates his point about misinformation. "All the bear experts say, 'A fed bear is a dead bear.' Wildlife officers tell people that once a bear learns to associate humans with food, it will start to hang around campsites and cause trouble until it eventually has to be destroyed. Well, I happen to know that bears are smart. They know where they're safe and where they're not safe. The average black bear in North America will be killed by a human before it is five years old. Bears get hit by cars and shot by hunters and peppered with bird shot by homeowners who don't want them around. The biggest old bear around here is blind and permanently infected in one eye because some guy gave him a 'warning shot' for eating dandelions on his front lawn. Black bears are fearful animals at the best of times, and they're really afraid of people. They don't like barking dogs and they don't like getting yelled at. The bears that come to my feeder know I appreciate them. They use a secretive trail to get here, and they stay out of sight when they're anywhere near built-up areas or highways. They're not stupid. They don't assume that just because I feed them, everybody else is going to feed them. Their attitude is, 'It's safe at Lynn's house, but don't push your luck with the others.'"

The next day, I go to witness the culmination of Lynn Rogers' lifework—the North American Bear Center, a non-profit, educational organization whose home is on the outskirts of Ely. It opened in May 2007, thanks to an army of volunteers and several million dollars in donations, no small part of which came from Lynn Rogers' own life savings. The Bear Center is a large building with the rather bland-looking, poured-concrete facade of an auto parts warehouse, but its plain design belies its lush and well-lit interior. (As Rogers later explains, "We wanted to spend our money inside, where it counts.") The walls are covered with murals depicting wild animals in natural settings. Life-sized mounts of black bears and grizzly bears are dwarfed by the skeleton of a short-faced bear, which dominates the main hall and gives a sense of the fearsome beast that ruled North America not very long ago and probably ate grizzlies as appetizers. Scattered around the building are exhibits, interactive displays and more than thirty wall-mounted televisions, each showing a different film of bears interacting in natural settings. Bird song, the rustle of running water and the purring of young bears nursing from their mothers provide a pleasant soundtrack to the educational exhibits. In the rear of the building, natural light pours in through a wall of floor-to-ceiling windows overlooking a forest glade with a pond and waterfall.

The glade and its large, two-acre forest enclosure are inhabited by Ted, Honey and Lucky—the centre's living exhibits. Lucky, the youngest bear of the trio, was born in 2007 and "adopted" by some people who pulled him from his den. When Lucky became too much to handle, they turned him over to the Wisconsin Department of Natural Resources, which in turn gave him to the Bear Center. Ted and Honey are ten years older than Lucky. Both were born in captivity and likewise became too much of a liability to their owners. Ted is an enormous, good-natured bear that makes happy tongue-clicking sounds when humans enter his enclosure. When Rogers arrives, he goes into the enclosure with Ted, and the big bear immediately stands up, hugs Rogers and licks his face. When I ask Rogers if I can go in and meet Ted and the other bears, he says that Honey, the female of the trio, doesn't like strangers. "Even though Honey grew up with Ted, she has a very different personality," he says, "which really shows how bears are all individuals. She gets blustery and sometimes bluff-charges anyone who enters the enclosure. It took her six months to trust me enough to allow me to come close to her. And when Lucky first arrived, she chased him up a tree."

Rogers says that, despite the teachings of many bear experts, young bears do not have to be educated about how to survive in the woods. "You can take a bear that grew up in captivity, and it will quickly learn to forage on wild plants as effectively as a bear that grew up in the wilds. Bears learn many things from their mothers, but they don't need to be taught what to eat. Their noses are superb for finding edible plants. They use their noses to home in on the plants and their eyes to focus on the food close up. And despite what most people think, bears are not colour-blind. They need colour vision in order to differentiate the different types of berries and plants, and that's why they sleep during the darkest part of the night. As soon as it's light enough to distinguish colour, they get up and start feeding again. When I'm following a bear in the woods and keeping it company, I try to sleep lightly so that I'll wake up when it wakes up. But sometimes the bear will get up around three in the morning and go off feeding, and I'll have a dickens of a time finding it."

Rogers and the other caretakers work with veterinarians and other experts to make sure the enclosure is well supplied with the kind of natural forage that bears prefer in the wild. He says Hollywood and the media like to portray bears as meat-eating predators, but in fact plants make up the bulk of their diet. "If you made a list of a black bear's top twenty preferred foods, meat would not even make the list." The enclosure is also designed to make the foraging process as stimulating as possible. "In the wild, bears are always moving, exploring the terrain, and to imitate that environment we try to make them 'work' for their food. It keeps them mentally sharp, physically active and curious."

They may be physically active, but Ted, the patriarch, still has that trademark look of a captive bear—the wide load, the sleepy demeanour, the fur as worn as a hotel carpet. The movie industry will sometimes employ bears as stock villains, cajoling them with food rewards to rear up and snarl in a melodramatic manner. But no one who has spent time in the woods would ever mistake an old tub of lard like Ted for a wild bear. His enclosure may be the best-designed bear installation in the world, but he still looks like a domesticated animal, and there's a world of difference between him and the trim, lustrous wild bear that came to Lynn Rogers' deck last night and walked the length of the railing like a house cat. To paraphrase Mark Twain, the difference between Ted and a wild bear is like the difference between the lightning bug and the lightning.

After Ted waddles off to take a nap, Rogers and I walk through the facility and he shows me some of the exhibits. The children's playroom has posters, books, bear games and a large-screen TV that continuously plays video footage of a wild black bear digging a rock out of the ground. The same rock sits in the playroom so kids can try to lift it and test their strength against a bear's. In the adult section, visitors can push buttons to hear different grunts, clicks and purring sounds, each one meaning something in bear language.

Another exhibit consists of an archive of large *Outdoor Life* magazine covers mounted on poster board, most of which depict growling bears up on their hind legs, smashing their way through cabin windows and joyously ripping hunters to pieces. "The snarling, growling bear has been a staple of hunting-magazine cover art for over a century," says Rogers. "Men in our culture don't have dragons they can go out and do battle with. The bear lives in the dark forest and symbolizes all the scary things that little boys are afraid of, so the bear has become our modern-day dragon. But any experienced outdoorsman knows that bears are not out to cause trouble. The media spread so much nonsense about bears. For example, you always hear newspaper accounts where a bear is 'growling.' But bears don't growl. The growl is simply not a part of bear vocabulary."

"How do they express aggression?"

Rogers pauses a beat before answering. Like most bear biologists, he is not entirely comfortable with the word "aggression," a word that subtly transfers human blame onto the bear. In his view, so-called bear aggression is actually just bears defending themselves. "A bear might slam its front feet on the ground or blow air explosively. And it will sometimes charge. But that's because it's afraid of you. Before it comes at you, it will lay its ears back to make its muzzle look narrow and elongated. We did a lot of work, provoking charges, trying to determine if they are the prelude to attack or simply a bluff. We have some of those tests on film here. Afterwards, you can go over to the monitor there and watch the footage. The clips are quite comical, as you'll see. As soon as the researcher stops running away, the bear immediately goes through contortions trying to halt the pursuit. In one case this bear practically turns a somersault in an attempt to avoid touching the researcher. The bottom line is that bluff charges are not aggressive. They are simply an expression of the bear's fear. The bear wants you to go away."

"Have you ever been nervous when you're out in the woods in the middle of the night and you run into a large, unfamiliar bear?"

He chuckles. "In the middle of the night there are only two things in the woods I'm afraid of—a mossy log and a sharp twig. You can slip on a mossy log and break your ankle. And a sharp twig can jab you in the eye and blind you."

This is all very persuasive—his positive attitude, his displays of button-eyed teddy bears, the tranquil music of the waterfall and the school kids exclaiming in delight as they watch films of bears cavorting in the meadow. It brings to mind all those old paintings and the charming, idealistic theories of Jean-Jacques Rousseau, the eighteenth-century French philosopher who believed that nature is an ideal realm where wild animals coexist in dynamic balance and where *Homo sapiens,* the "noble savage," is at his purest state. You can't spend much time with Lynn Rogers without thinking that this loping, enthusiastic sixty-seven-year-old is the sort of man Rousseau would have admired. Given that Rogers is not a philosopher, but a rough-and-tumble scientist who has earned his opinions with a lifetime of travel and exploration in the wilderness, one is tempted to assume that everything you need to know about black bears is enclosed within his brain. But as we all know, the Peaceable Kingdom is not always peaceful, and even Rogers seems a bit stumped when you summon the temerity to ask him why black bears sometimes kill human beings. "No one really knows," he says. "It's very rare."

"What's the most dangerous type of black bear?"

"Black bears that kill people are usually large, healthy males."

"Why do they attack people?"

Rogers frowns. It's easy to see that he doesn't enjoy talking about this. "Fatal black bear attacks are usually predatory in nature," he says. "But it's very, very uncommon, and it usually involves a wilderness bear that has never seen a person before."

"Have you ever experienced that sort of predatory behaviour?"

He smiles. "I've interacted with literally thousands of bears at close range and never felt threatened in any way. I'm not saying there is no such thing as a predatory black bear. I just haven't met one yet."

Man-Eaters

Joan Robinson was at church one Sunday morning when a man approached and asked if he could sit down. She was sixty-three years old at the time, a divorced Winnipeg real estate agent accustomed to supporting herself, and was not looking to change her single status. But something about this man drew her interest. "He was an older man," she says. "I thought he was much too old for me. But for the rest of the service, I found myself glancing at his hands. He obviously worked outdoors, because he had these strong, tanned hands. It was the oddest thing, because as I sat there looking at his hands, I felt the Lord speak to me, saying, 'I have sent this man to be your mate.'"

Six months later they were married. Harvey Robinson owned a farm near Selkirk, a short drive north of Winnipeg. Joan was a city girl, but it seemed to make sense to move out to Harvey's farm. "It was a bit of a transition at first," she says. "I went from high heels to rubber boots." But Harvey's home was more like a suburban home than a farm—a modern ranch house next to a busy highway. Surrounded by prairie and protected from the winter winds by mature woods, it offered the best of both worlds. Just a few miles to the north the prairie ended and the great northern forest began—a land of blue lakes, good berry picking and the white sand beaches of Lake Winnipeg. To the south, the city was so close Joan could almost see the skyline from her yard. She could go shopping in the department stores and supermarkets of Winnipeg in the afternoon and be back home half an hour later, making dinner and looking out the window at the deer grazing in her yard. They raised chickens, sheep, goats and cattle. The head of the herd was a bull named Gabriel, and they gave his calves biblical names. "Harvey handled the big animals," she says. "And that was okay with me because they scared me. We divided up all the work by our personal preference. Harvey liked picking gooseberries, saskatoons and raspberries in the woods behind the house, and I liked making jams and preserves. He did most of the outside work, and I ran the house."

One day a pregnant cow got out and wandered back into the woodlot to have her calf. Harvey brought them back and, over dinner, told Joan that during the search he'd discovered a motherlode of wild plums along a fence just a few hundred yards behind the house. It was a dry year and the blueberry crop had failed, but the plums seemed to prosper with all the sunlight. Harvey said that he wanted to go and pick the plums the next day. "This wasn't exactly exciting news," Joan says. "I had been making jam all summer and I was getting a bit tired of it. I should have told Harvey I needed a break from jamming, but I let it pass. So the next morning, off he went to pick the plums. Harvey was an active man and he ate three big meals a day, so I planned to have a good lunch waiting for him when he got back with his buckets of plums. He was also very punctual, so I expected him back for lunch at twelve noon sharp."

All morning, Joan tried to work, but she felt dispirited. "It felt like something was wrong. I can't explain it. There was a kind of heaviness on me. I tried to cut the grass, but it just made me feel worried. I looked forward to seeing Harvey at noon, but he was late, and right away I was worried even more—not just because of the dreadful way I'd felt all morning, but because he was never late. I honked the car horn and rang the cowbell, but there was no sign of him. I was recovering from a hip replacement and I wasn't strong enough to go back in the woods looking for him. There are holes in the ground back there, and I was worried that maybe he'd fallen and hurt himself. So after about forty-five minutes of waiting, I decided to get help. I didn't want to call the police because I thought they would just dismiss me. But I didn't know what else to do."

Joan telephoned the Royal Canadian Mounted Police. Constable Stan Mozdzen was at his desk when the call came in. Mozdzen is a chipper, fit-looking guy in his thirties who grew up on a farm in southern Manitoba. On duty, he wears all the combat gear of a modern front-line cop: the heavy boots, the snug ballistic vest and the tactical belt bristling with weaponry— asp, pepper spray, cuffs and pistol. But you can't take the manners out of a farm boy, and Mozdzen has the direct, open face of a guy who has seen a lot of bad things but still likes to look on the bright side. "I was doing some paperwork at my desk when Carol came in and told me this lady had called and reported that her husband hadn't come home for lunch. I was pretty busy but I said okay, I'll drive over and have a look."

Fetching his car keys, Stan slaps on his hat and we go out to the parking lot, where the sun is beating on the rows of police cars. It's a steamy, hot day and the asphalt is spongy underfoot. The sky is white and the prairie wind redolent with the smell of newly mown alfalfa and the rainstorms predicted for later today. It was just like this last year, when Joan's call came in, so without exactly meaning to, we're recreating the day it happened. Like most Mounties, Stan works alone, so it wouldn't have been unusual for him to answer the call by himself. Driving over to the farm, he tells me about his typical workload. Selkirk is a prosperous small town with good schools and strong community spirit. But there's no such thing as a quiet policing job. Like any modern town, Selkirk has its share of drug problems, sexual assaults, domestic homicides, fatal car accidents, gory suicides and garden-variety criminal monkey business. It has taken us two months of calling back and forth to find a place in his timetable for this outing, but even though he's had to cancel a couple of times, he has always called back and rescheduled. The single-mindedness with which he handles his job is evidenced when we happen upon a car accident en route to the farm. Someone has gone through a yellow light and T-boned someone else. Radiator fluid, glass and plastic car parts are scattered across the road. Two men are arguing with each other, pointing at the traffic light and bemoaning their shattered vehicles. They both lock their eyes with relief on Stan's approaching car, but he cruises right past— sorry folks, one job at a time.

For a few minutes we drive along a busy highway, then Stan turns down a gravel road and eases up a driveway into a farmyard. "The emergency vehicles had difficulty finding this place," he says. "That's typical of life in the country. Everybody knows where they're going, so they never get around to putting up signs."

Parking the police car in the driveway, Stan says he wants to talk to the new homeowners to ask permission to visit the scene. Leaning against the hot fender of the car, I shoo away horseflies as Stan confers with a man for a few minutes in the foyer of the house. Dark police uniforms make no concessions to the summer heat, and when Stan returns, his face is shiny with perspiration. "No problem at all," he says. "Let's go for a walk and I'll show you where it happened."

Taking a pump-action shotgun out of the car, Stan says, "If you don't mind, I'm going to bring this along. I didn't have it with me last summer and I'd feel better carrying it."

He says that last year, when he was talking to Joan and taking her information about Harvey's disappearance, her step-son showed up to help. Stan and the stepson agreed to split up and walk around the property. We go walking into the woods. Stan hasn't been back here since, and it occurs to me that he's a bit distracted, going through a fairly intense reliving of the events of that day. After a short distance the trail opens up into a hay-field. He pauses, looks across the field and says, "Okay, so I was standing here, thinking maybe he'd been working on a piece of equipment and got caught underneath. We see that happen to farmers sometimes. I was also thinking that maybe he'd had a stroke and was wandering around in confusion. I certainly wasn't thinking bear."

There would be no reason for him to think bear. There are no grizzlies in southern Manitoba, and attacks by black bears are rare.* It was particularly inconceivable given the time and location—twenty minutes from downtown Winnipeg, in broad daylight, with open fields all around and highway traffic whizzing past. Stan says he always considered black bears to be shy, fearful animals, and though in recent years they have been sighted more frequently in the woods around Selkirk, he had never heard of one attacking a person. So he continued his search, expecting to find Harvey disabled from an injury of some kind, when his cell phone rang. It was Joan, telling him that her stepson had found Harvey's hat, a bloody knife and some spilled plums. Stan said, "Tell him to stay where he is."

Stan hurried over to the spot. Joan's stepson had been joined by some other volunteer searchers. They were standing in the field, next to a large flattened-down area. Things always look a little different when you return a year later, and today, Stan walks up and down the fenceline a few times until he is certain of the exact location. "The flattened-down spot was right here," he finally says, leading me through the tangled, knee-high canola to a place about ten yards from the fence. He squats down and sorts through the grass where the knife had been lying. "It didn't look right. I still wasn't thinking about a wild animal. I was thinking that maybe he'd stumbled onto a marijuana grow operation and there'd been a fight. In any case, I knew we needed to back out of there until we got some reinforcements. I called the corporal and told him we needed a dog master out here and a couple of more officers."

---

* When you consider that there are 750,000 black bears in North America, the number of bad apples in the bear population is low indeed. Every year only one or two of those bears will kill a person. During the same time period, about one out of fifty thousand people will commit murder.

The corporal advised him that help was on the way. They began retreating, the volunteers and Joan's stepson walking ahead, when Stan spotted a beaten-down trail leading from the scene. "The grass was packed down and bent over, like something had been dragged that way."

He started following the trail, walked a few steps into the bush and froze in his tracks. "Just ahead of me I saw Harvey lying face down over a log." He approached cautiously. Harvey had been scalped, and enough time had passed that the blood on his skull was dry and black. His jeans were soaked with blood and the muscles of his shoulders had been torn away, showing white skeleton. Harvey was long dead, but out of habit Stan knelt down to check his carotid artery for a pulse. Then there was a crashing noise, and a large animal jumped up about six yards away. "It was a black bear," he says. "It must have been sleeping next to Harvey's body. As soon as it became aware of my presence it jumped up and ran away. I pulled my sidearm and yelled at the other guys to leave the area because there was a bear. The bear ran about ten yards in a kind of semicircle, then stopped and looked at me. I could see its black ears pointing up above the underbrush."

Stan and I are standing now in the bush, at the place where Harvey's body was lying, and Stan is pointing to the place where the bear stopped. The air is still and hot in these woods, with interlaced dead saplings lying everywhere. If you made a quick move in any direction you'd probably trip over a stick and go down like a sack of potatoes. Stan stares at the place where the bear was. "The bear was making a kind of wheezing noise, but it wasn't snarling or growling. I took a step backward, and suddenly it came at me in a full charge."

A bluff charge from a black bear is usually preceded by posturing and threats—the bear will swat the ground, blow air, lower its head, slick back its ears and click its teeth before making its rush. But bluff charges almost never conclude with physical contact. Unlike grizzlies, black bears are not known for physically defending their food caches, personal space or cubs. Scientists have learned they can handle cubs while the mother bear observes meekly from a distance, and most black bears, especially those that have become familiar with hunters, quickly beat a retreat when they encounter a human in the woods.

Attacks in which the bear makes contact with a human are unusual, and they are classed as either defensive or offensive. Defensive attacks usually involve habituated bears that have lost their fear of humans, and these attacks are usually minor. Typically, a defensive attack involves a campground bear swatting or "message biting" a human who has tried to drive it away from a source of food. Offensive or predatory attacks are much more serious. Bears in predatory mode do not posture aggressively, blow air or slap the ground with their paws. They move quietly and purposefully towards their intended victim, sometimes following a hiker or forestry worker for some distance through the woods before closing in.

Predatory attacks are rare, but they make a strong impression on people who experience them. There's something about the idea of being hunted by a wild animal that arouses ancient and deeply seated horrors in the human psyche. The same year that Harvey Robinson was killed, predatory bears killed two other people in North America. In one case, a seventy-one-year-old tourist outfitter named Merlyn Carter flew up to his family's fishing lodge on Nonacho Lake, Northwest Territories, to prepare it for the first guests of the season. The next morning, his wife, Jean, and son Myles flew up to the lodge, landed their float plane, taxied up to the dock and became concerned when Merlyn wasn't there to greet them. When Jean went up the path to look for him, a black bear appeared and chased her down to the dock. Myles hit the bear with a length of steel dock ramp and it retreated. Myles went up to the lodge to fetch a rifle. He spotted the bear behind the lodge, shot it three times and killed it. It was lying next to the half-eaten remains of his father.

A few weeks after Harvey Robinson was killed, a pretty thirty-year-old doctor named Jacqueline Perry was kayaking with her husband, Marc Jordan, at a remote lake near Chapleau, Ontario. While they were making camp, a black bear came out of the bush and attacked Jacqueline. The bear dragged her screaming towards the woods. Marc jumped on the bear and stabbed it with a Swiss Army knife. Bleeding from the neck, the bear dropped her and attacked Marc. He fought it off long enough to load Jacqueline into their kayak and paddle off, screaming for help. The area is remote wilderness, but his cries were eventually heard by two other campers, who had had bear problems of their own earlier that day. Her wounds were horrific, and by the time a doctor arrived she was dead.

Three black bear fatalities in one summer are a little high, but not far out of the normal range. In an average summer, black and grizzly bears kill three people in North America. Grizzlies are more aggressive, and they account for more fatal attacks, but grizzlies can cite extenuating circumstances. Modern justice systems take into account the perpetrator's state of mind, and in most cases a grizzly can plead self-defence. The most dangerous bear in the woods might be a female grizzly with cubs, but we all have a soft spot for the pressures of motherhood, and rightly or wrongly, an aggressive sow grizzly is acting only out of a determination to protect her offspring. In a sow grizzly's mind, any large mammal that approaches her intends to harm her cubs, and this is not an unreasonable belief since male grizzlies will attack cubs any time they get a chance. A sow grizzly is no match for a big male, but her furious determination to protect her cubs is so explosive that the average boar just can't see the upside. Human beings, not unreasonably, are seen as an equal threat. Once she chases off the other bear or neutralizes the human intruder, she rounds up her cubs and runs away. Black bears, on the other hand, don't usually behave aggressively in defence of their cubs, food or territory. That's the good news. The bad news is that, unlike grizzlies, they sometimes kill people for food. And man-eating animals are the stuff of nightmares. Despite Lynn Rogers' conviction that newspapers love to sensationalize, one might also argue that papers and the news media in general seem rather prim when it comes to reporting the details of predatory black bear attacks. Usually, the attack is described as a "mauling"—a hoary journalistic cliché that evokes a dumb, well-meaning beast rolling around with someone on the ground and perhaps dispatching them with over-ardent hugs and liberal applications of slobber. In fact, predatory black bears usually tackle the victim, administer an expert paralyzing bite to the neck then begin stripping off as much meat as they can gulp down.

Predatory bear attacks are increasing in frequency. And although attacks tend to be more common when natural food crops fail, the general rise in the number of attacks is not well understood. According to world-famous bear scientist Stephen Herrero of the University of Calgary, 128 people were killed by grizzly and black bears in North America during the twentieth century—slightly more than one per year, but averages are misleading because there was only one fatal bear attack in the 1930s and six in the 1940s. Fifty-six of the victims on the list, or nearly half, were killed in the last twenty years. "There is a definite upward trend in bear-inflicted injuries," Dr. Herrero says. "It really began taking off in the 1980s."

There are two schools of thought about the increase. Bear enthusiasts and environmentalists tend to blame human beings, arguing that beleaguered bears are getting crowded by more and more people invading their habitat. Dissenters, many of whom are bush workers, outfitters and backwoods types, tend to blame the bears, saying that in fact there are more bears than ever, and restrictions placed on hunting seasons and firearm ownership have encouraged the animals to behave with impunity around humans. Some experts suggest that we not only have more people but more bears. Other experts point out the obvious—that one explanation might be valid in one region, and another might be valid in a different place. Northern British Columbia, for example, is sparsely populated by humans but is a recurring trouble spot for predatory black bear attacks. In one gruesome case, a black bear attacked and killed a thirty-seven-year-old mother from Paris, Texas, at a popular hot springs in northern B.C. as her two children wept and screamed for help. The bear then killed a would-be rescuer, injured the woman's thirteen-year-old son when he tried to save her, and mangled a fourth rescuer before another camper who had a rifle in his truck managed to kill it. If he hadn't, the body count might have been even higher.

"Aggressive black bears are common in northern B.C.," says bear expert Gary Shelton. "I know there's never been a fatal black bear attack in Minnesota, where Lynn Rogers does most of his research, but in my opinion that's because of their diet. The bears in Minnesota live on berries, insects and plant matter. The black bears in northern B.C. cope with long winters and short summers, and there isn't as much in the way of plant food. If a northern bear wants to put on enough weight to survive the winter, he has to include predation in his survival strategy. He has to hunt moose calves and whatever else he can pull down. I'm sure Lynn Rogers is safe sleeping on the ground next to Minnesota black bears, but he might not last long if he attempted that up here."

Bear attacks are only recorded as "attacks" when a human is killed or hospitalized. No accounting is made of incidents where a predatory bear is scared off by a prospective victim. Those just become more "bear stories," of which there is no shortage in the backcountry. Talk to any hunter, camper or forestry worker in northern British Columbia, and they will probably have an anecdote about the time they had a near-miss with a black bear. Rick Hansen, for example, had a typical encounter—no blood, no physical contact, but a lingering sense that he might have had a close call. Hansen, a famous wheelchair athlete, was disabled when he was fifteen years old. He was hitch-hiking home from a fishing trip with his friends when he was picked up by a drunken driver, who proceeded to roll the vehicle. Hansen's back was broken. For the first few years, he had a hard time accepting that he was going to spend the rest of his life in a wheelchair, but his brother Brad dragged him along on a fishing trip with their father, and Hansen rediscovered his zest for life. "I realized that if I could still fish, maybe I could do other things too." He began working out with weights, entered university and became the first disabled person to graduate from the University of

British Columbia with a degree in physical education. He then won nineteen international wheelchair marathons and competed for Canada in the wheelchair events at the 1984 Olympics in Los Angeles. In 1985 he embarked on a round-the-world trip in his wheelchair, covering forty thousand kilometres and eventually raising more than $200 million for spinal cord injury research. Fishing and hunting expeditions with his family and friends are still an important part of his life. Hansen told me that last year, he was moose hunting at his favourite place in northern British Columbia when he ran into a "spooky" bear.

"I was sitting at an intersection of two cutlines when this very large black bear walked out of the woods about forty feet away. I've seen a lot of bears, and they're usually quite timid. But this one just stared at me, and there was something about his attitude that was really unsettling. The best way I can describe it is spooky. He just had a weird look in his eye. He circled around and came up behind me, looking at me the whole time, and I was beginning to think I might have a real problem when the bear seemed to change his mind and just melted away into the bush."

Hansen, a paraplegic, was unable to retreat or make any abrupt moves, and that might have worked in his favour, since the evidence suggests that a solid, resolute stance is the best deterrent to an aggressive bear. He was also armed with a heavy rifle, so he would have been able to knock the animal down if it had come too close. In cases like that, the individual never knows what might have happened in different circumstances. Maybe the bear was just curious. Thinking about it afterwards, who's to know? Bears can be so hard to read that it's difficult to distinguish a slightly odd encounter with a confident but harmless bear from a close brush with a truly dangerous animal.

Lillian Anderson, a biologist with the Ontario Ministry of Natural Resources in Kenora, Ontario, is an author and nature lover who camps, fishes and hunts with her husband, Bruce, and rehabilitates injured pelicans, hawks and other injured birds at her home. Lillian knows more about wild animals than any woman I know, and she believes that most black bears are shy, intelligent animals that ordinarily go out of their way to avoid trouble. But last year she met a bear that behaved differently from the others. Lillian was walking her dogs along the bush road near their house when a large black bear came out of the bush. "I've never encountered a bear that behaved like this," says Lillian. "It went into full predatory mode, like a cat stalking a bird. This bear was so plainly bent on attacking us that even the dogs were frightened. I began backing up, yelling at the bear, and did anything I could do to intimidate it. There was a long piece of steel angle iron on the side of the road. I picked it up and began beating on a culvert, yelling and just trying to show this bear how I was going to fight if it came any closer. I retreated slowly back to the house, beating the road with the steel bar, smacking the gravel, and yelling. The bear followed most of the way. If I hadn't happened upon that piece of angle iron, I don't know what would have happened, but the whole experience was really scary. I'm convinced that bear intended to kill me."

Consistent with first-hand accounts like Lillian Anderson's, predatory black bears usually follow their intended victim for a while, cautiously measuring them up for vulnerability before closing in. Bear experts therefore recommend using whatever tools are handy to intimidate the animal. If you are carrying pepper spray or a firearm, be prepared to use it. Do not speak softly or behave in a submissive manner. If the bear presses the attack,

do not run or fall on the ground and "play dead," as is often rec-
ommended in the case of grizzly attacks. As Gary Shelton says,
"If you play dead with a predatory black bear, you will probably
end up dead." Most bear experts recommend using any means at
your disposal to scare off the animal. Shout and threaten. Open
your jacket and spread it out to make yourself look larger. Pick
up a dead limb off the ground and thrash the bushes. If the bear
attacks, fight back with everything you have. Gouge its eyes. Stab
it with a knife. Bears have to weigh the benefits of a meal against
the possibility of being injured. Wild animals can't get access to
workers' compensation, and if they get badly hurt they're in serious trouble. "You usually have a bit of time. If you can convince
the bear that he is going to pay a high price for his meal," says
Shelton, "he will often back off."

Predatory black bears don't always give warning before
attacking. In 1996 a rancher in the Chilcotin district of British
Columbia was riding his horse when a black bear suddenly charged
him. He spurred the horse to get away but fell off and was killed
by the bear. In July 2000 a top-ranked Canadian biathlete named
Mary Beth Miller was jogging along a popular running trail near
Quebec City when a black bear jumped out of the woods and
tackled her. She broke free and kept running, but the bear caught
her and killed her.

In 2006 thirty-one-year-old Robin Kochorek went on an
eight-month-long adventure tour in which she visited twenty-five
countries. She was mugged in South America and carjacked in
South Africa. But her friends said she loved the whole experience,
and when she came home to Windermere, British Columbia, she
set about raising money for orphans she met during her travels.
Described by her brother Michael as a bubbly, passionate and

energetic young woman, Kochorek was looking forward to getting back to work as a speech pathologist, helping children with severe learning disabilities.

In late July of 2007, she went mountain-biking with some friends near Panorama ski resort in the mountains of eastern British Columbia, and ended up parting with her friends when they chose a difficult path down the mountain. She opted for a "safe route," not realizing that during the previous week several cyclists had been chased by an aggressive black bear along that same trail. (Local officials had decided not to post the trail with warning signs, a decision her brother calls "absurd." He says his sister was a sensible, cautious person who would never have taken that route had there been a sign warning hikers about an aggressive bear.) When she didn't return by evening, a search was launched. The next morning, the searchers stumbled upon a bear that was guarding Kochorek's half-eaten remains. The bear charged the searchers and was shot and killed by an RCMP officer.

Just as newspapers tend to be reticent about publishing the gruesome facts of predatory bear attacks, they never seem very good at ferreting out other crucial details of the story. What's it like when you meet the bear and it comes at a dead run? What goes through your mind? The newspapers usually refer to the moment of truth ("The bear was shot and killed by an RCMP officer") as a mere detail, as if dispatching a charging bear is no more difficult than flipping a light switch. According to the movies, you point a gun and *bang,* the bear falls over. But it doesn't work that way. Bears are hard to kill; they can live for several minutes with their hearts shot away. Wildlife officers, game wardens and other officials who have to cope with dangerous animals are usually equipped with magnum 12-gauge shotguns, which can deliver over a ton and a half of impact energy with each shot. Even with such formidable weapons, multiple shots are often required. In many cases, police officers are carrying only a sidearm, which is usually a nine-millimetre pistol that delivers a small, short-range bullet that hits with about one-tenth the force of a shotgun. To add to the danger, a running bear coming at full charge through broken undergrowth is a bouncing target that can cover thirty yards in two seconds. The bear that charged Constable Stan Mozdzen after killing Harvey Robinson was about half that distance away. "It's really hard to describe how fast they are," he says. "One second it was fifteen yards away; the next second it was right there."

Mozdzen had done a lot of target shooting and gopher hunting when he was a kid growing up on the farm, and his reaction was shaped by all those years of practice. "Time really does slow down in an emergency, and even though it only took a second or two, I was very conscious of raising the gun, saying to myself, 'Take your time and don't screw this up,' and getting the sights properly lined up on the bear's chest just under his chin before pulling the trigger. At the first shot he was about eight yards away, coming full speed. The gun recoiled, and by the time I got it levelled again and re-established my sight picture, he was about three yards and coming. I fired again, and at the impact of the bullet he spun around and ran off into the bush."

In a short time, the farm was deluged with emergency vehicles, police, wildlife officers, a helicopter and local citizen volunteers. They surrounded the woodlot, and a search party moved into the bush and found the bear lying dead about twenty yards from where Mozdzen had fired his pistol. Human flesh was found in its stomach, and the necropsy established that

Mozdzen's shooting had been unerring. One bullet had gone through its lungs, the other its liver. The bear was a full-grown male in relatively good health but quite skinny, about seventy pounds underweight. It would have had a poor chance of surviving the winter, and it probably knew it. "The government wildlife experts said the bear was having a hard time," says Mozdzen. "There weren't a lot of berries last year, and a bear under pressure from hunger will do things a bear won't normally do."

Stan and I are standing right at the spot where Harvey died, looking down at a wooden cross his family placed in his memory. Bears usually bed down in the heat of the day, and the bear was probably asleep when Harvey disturbed it. What happened next is hard to know, but it might have done the same thing it did when Stan disturbed it: run a few yards, stopped, looked at Harvey for a moment and charged him.

"We know Harvey put up a fight because the knife had bear blood on it," says Stan Mozdzen. "He didn't have much of a chance with a little knife, but he tried."

We stand in silence for a few minutes, sweltering in the heat of the tangled bush. There doesn't seem to be much else to add.

Stan drops me off back at the detachment, and I go and see Joan, who now lives in the town of Selkirk. She pours me a cup of tea and bustles around the kitchen fetching milk and sugar, not visibly upset by the prospect of talking about Harvey's death. "I was angry at the funeral," she says. "It was a closed coffin, so I knew Harvey must have suffered terribly before he died. But I've spoken to the Lord about it and I'm not angry anymore."

I'm wondering if Joan's equanimity has come with the passage of time, or whether she has drawn some kind of conclusion about wild animals that has helped her put Harvey's death in perspective. People like Lynn Rogers argue that bears are essentially harmless and that nature is the closest thing we have to the garden of Eden. That's what Jean-Jacques Rousseau wanted us to believe, and it's a compelling idea. But Rousseau didn't have much luck killing off the durable ideas of his old nemesis, the English philosopher Thomas Hobbes, who argued that, outside civilization, violence is the currency of survival and that life in nature is in fact "solitary, poor, nasty, brutish, and short."

One point of view is hawkish and the other pacifistic. One argument proposes a world that is essentially nice and the other, one that is nasty, or "red in tooth and claw." For centuries, our view of the natural world has yawed back and forth between the two opposites. You can't visit Lynn Rogers' Bear Center without being captivated by a cordial view of the natural world, and you can't look at the photographs of mangled human remains without suspecting that Hobbes had it right. As far as Joan Robinson is concerned, neither viewpoint gives the whole picture. When I ask her if she hates bears now, she says, "They're all God's creatures. When I see a bear, I still think, 'My goodness, what a majestic and beautiful animal.' I don't dislike bears because of what happened to Harvey."

She places a platter of cookies on the table and sits down. "That poor animal was starving," she says. "He was just being a bear."

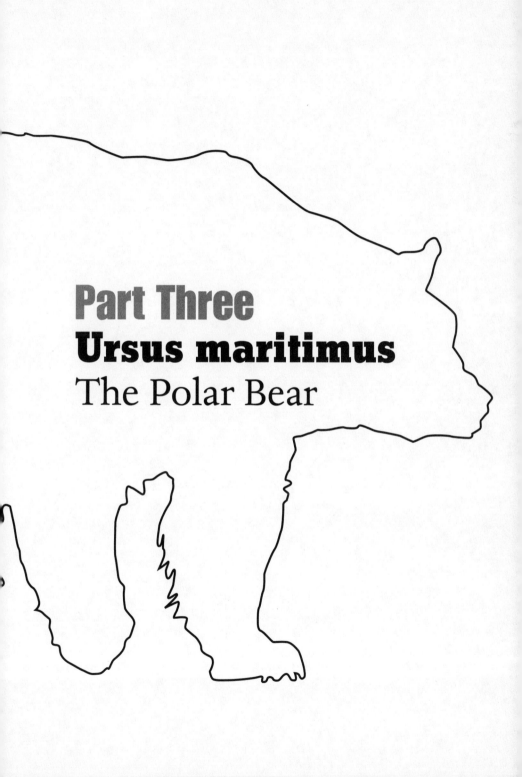

Part Three
Ursus maritimus
The Polar Bear

Land of the
Snow Walker

After a long journey into the wilderness, the lurching of the train and the tooting of the whistle announce that we're finally rolling into Churchill, Manitoba. The conductor walks through the car and informs us that we'll be stopping in ten minutes. I'm sitting in the dining car with the other members of my tour group—mostly Brits and Americans who have come up here to look at polar bears—and one of them jokingly asks the conductor if a bear will be waiting for us when we get off the train.

"There were two big ones right by the station last week," the conductor says. "The engineer had to blow the whistle to shoo them off the tracks."

A ripple of excitement sweeps through the car. Polar bears were right at the train station! Everyone rushes back to their rooms to get their bags and cameras. The waitress is smiling as she picks up their plates. She's been on this run dozens of times and knows how giddy people get when they're about to meet *Ursus maritimus*. Heading back to my car, I walk with a crooked-kneed gait, prepared to be knocked off balance at any moment by the funhouse shuffling of the train. For the last eighteen hours the train has been humping over the permafrost and rolling sideways like a sailboat in heavy swells. We've spent two nights on the train, and once we crossed the northern frost line, the roadbed went to pot. Some of the tour group members complained over breakfast that the train pitched and heaved so vigorously during the night that they were unable to sleep. But I've used the old sailor's trick of jamming my body against the bulkhead with knapsacks and pillows. All night long, the berth vaulted and swayed to the syncopated backbeat of the wheels. At one point, I sat up, looked out the window and saw a blazing silver moon shining down on the snow. Spruce trees paraded by, interspersed with open muskeg bogs, and I had the odd reassuring sense of being safe and cozy without having a clue where we were.

On a train the obligation to pee is the downside of having that nightcap before bed. My roomette had a toilet, but in order to complete the operation I would have had to climb out into the aisle and fold the bed back into the wall to get access to the toilet. It would have been a five-minute procedure, so I just got dressed and headed down the hall to the public washroom. The train was utterly deserted and it felt late. The waitress in the bar car told me that Europeans—Germans in particular—don't bother with getting dressed when they walk down to the public toilet. More than once, she's closed the bar and headed down to her roomette and collided with a large, hairy, balls-naked German. The aisle is narrow, and she says there's always a bit of eye-rolling and a strained smile as they squeeze past each other.

Travel by train also makes a person (me, anyway) feel a little guilty about spending a couple of days doing nothing much except looking out the window. My self-inflicted work ethic is always whispering in my ear, suggesting that I should have taken the plane so that I could spend these days more "effectively"— such as staring at a computer screen and cranking out product. There's daily air service to Churchill, and it takes only about two hours from Winnipeg, and I could have been there by now. But air travel has become a form of fax transmission for humans. You feed your body into the machine and pop out at the other end. It might be cheaper and easier, but it's Faust's bargain. Travelling north by train is slow, but it's the only way to absorb the enormous swath of wilderness between the southern prairies and the northern coastal barrens where the polar bears live. When you ride the train, overturning the efficiencies of air travel by more or less doing nothing for two days—reading a novel, going for lunch, having a nap, reading some more, sitting in the silence of your roomette and looking out the window at the great forests rolling by, then, finally, around five in the afternoon, when the autumn light is fading and the woods are growing dark, adjourning to the bar car and having a beer with the trappers and miners and gabby eccentrics who are always in good supply on any backwoods train—you have a much better chance of experiencing those interesting moments that used to be called life. The highest praise you can give an air journey is to say that you didn't have to talk to your seatmate and nothing happened. A train journey feels random and social and unpredictable, as travel is supposed to be. When we left Winnipeg, I didn't know a soul on this train. Now six or eight of them feel like old friends. When we left Winnipeg, the leaves were falling and it was Indian summer. Now, as we approach the outskirts of Churchill, it's daybreak; the sun is flooding across the land, and the large windows reveal a harsh wintry landscape— endless tundra, scalloped snowdrifts and small clumps of scraggly spruces hunched against the wind.

Hauling my bags to the front of the train, I join the rest of the group. After a flurry of whistles from the locomotive, the train glides to a stop and the conductor opens the doors. Climbing down onto the platform, we mill around in the sharp cold, shivering, stamping our feet and waiting for our tour guide to materialize. Churchill is a small town—basically, a village. But like the Okavango Delta in Africa or the Monteverde cloud forest in Costa Rica, it has become a mandatory stop on the global adventure route for ecotourists. Churchill is about the same size as Bella Coola, but instead of treating its wandering bears as dangerous nuisances, it has turned them into tourist attractions. It's a mixed blessing, having ten or fifteen thousand bear gawkers arriving here every autumn, but it has undeniably been good for business. During bear season, which generally runs from Labour Day to Halloween, every hotel room, airline seat and train ticket is sold out far in advance. Large tour companies monopolize most of the hotel rooms, so you don't have much choice but to sign up with a tour group. My tour guide is a cute but bossy redhead who looks to be about the same age as my daughter. Checking our names on her clipboard, she herds us towards a school bus. Apparently, we're not allowed to take our luggage, so there's some last-minute panic as the members of our group dig through their bags, trying to find mitts, cameras and packets of Imodium. She explains that she has already made reservations for our dinner, and our luggage will be sent on to our hotel, so our only responsibility is not to wander off. This is all very pleasant, if a bit infantilizing. Packaged tours relieve you of the necessity of hauling your luggage around, but they also give you a preview of what it will be like when you get old.

We all march onto the bus for an introductory drive through Churchill. Our tour boss provides commentary as we bump along the main street and down to the grain-loading terminal. Near the grain pier, we all dismount and aim our binoculars at the bleak stony coastline. Ice slabs as thick as flatcars are littered on the rocky shoreline. Forty feet away, a sign is impaled in a snowbank: POLAR BEAR ALERT—DO NOT WALK IN THIS AREA. Adjusting my binoculars, I spot an Arctic fox skipping down the shore, weightless as a goose feather. Then, high above the grain terminal, a trio of birds twirl and skirmish. Two of the birds display the unmistakable soaring flight and broad-tailed silhouette of ravens. But the third, above them, is a quicker flier and appears to be attacking them. Nudging the folks beside me, I draw their attention to the aerial drama. I've been to the Arctic on half a dozen occasions, but this is the first time I've seen a gyrfalcon. The dogfight between them continues unresolved, and eventually they pirouette towards the high towers of the grain terminal, where they disappear from sight.

Climbing back into the bus, we trundle off to the Eskimo Museum. En route, Miss Bossy offers the floor to another guide, a biologist from a conservation group called Polar Bears International. Showing us an enormous bear skull, she gives us a brief lecture on the history and evolutionary development of polar bears. There's something about polar bears that excites curiosity and fear in almost everyone, and I immediately realize I have to get myself one of those skulls. When I was a small boy, I spent many hours drawing bears—bears looking indomitable on crags of ice, bears rearing above snow houses, bears surrounded by baying dogs, and bears fighting with Arctic fur trappers, great scribbles of Crayola red spewing across the page as the noble beast sent someone's head flying. My father had a large library of hefty, well-illustrated animal books, and I read them from cover to cover. I knew that polar bears evolved from "brown bears," which is the scientific catch-all term for grizzlies, Kodiaks, Russian brown bears, Alaskan brown bears, European brown bears and even those bike-riding circus bears in party hats. Scientifically speaking, they are all the same animal. The size and behaviour of brown bears is shaped by what they eat, where they live and how they've learned to cope. If you go back a little way (about two hundred thousand years), the northern hemisphere of the planet was covered with ice. Even in summer, a mile-thick slab of ice covered almost all of what is now Canada. Large mammals like bears, bison, mammoths and dire wolves roamed the Barren Lands and spruce forests along the southern fringes of this vast domain of ice.

Glaciers don't necessarily move at a glacial pace. They can bulldoze their way forward as quickly as a hundred yards a day, and according to scientific theory, some of these brown bears were hemmed in and isolated by a migrating glacier. Brown bears need to consume tens of thousands of calories a day in order to survive, and most of them would have had trouble finding that much food in the rocky areas of the northern coast. But in every litter of cubs there is evolutionary variability, and some young bears would have been better equipped than others to cope with the ice-bound conditions. These adaptable bears would have scrounged a living from carrion, stranded whales and any seals and walruses they could catch. Some of them would have been better at hunting than others, and these bears would have been favoured by evolution to breed and pass on their genes. Animals can evolve very quickly—look at the many breeds of dogs that have evolved in only a few hundred years—and the wintry conditions would have favoured bears with pale coloration, heavy fur and stalking skills. Continuing refinements to these evolutionary benefits would have sent the isolated brown bears down the road towards becoming what we now call polar bears.*

These new coastal bears developed flat, snowshoe-like paws, white fur and long, hooked teeth to better suit their new jobs as predators. If you examine a polar bear skull, you see evidence of an animal adapted for hunting. Predators tend to have forward-facing eyes. (As do humans, which is one of the reasons prey species like deer and rabbits—which have side-mounted eyes that enable them to look to the rear—instinctively recognize us as trouble.) The polar bear's eyes are aimed forward. The front canine teeth are as strong and thick as the prongs on an ice axe, and the lower teeth jut out beneath the uppers, making the jaw look underslung and vaguely saurian, like the maw of a smallish

---

* Even today, the two sometimes interbreed. In 2006 an American hunter accompanied by Inuit guides shot a white bear on the southern tip of Banks Island in the Canadian Arctic. On close examination, the bear seemed to have grizzly-like features—long claws, a hump above the shoulders and a dished face. DNA tests confirmed that the bear was a hybrid, and locals argued over whether it should be called a "grolar bear" or a "pizzly." Government officials were not amused and charged the hunter with shooting a grizzly, or at least half a grizzly, without a permit.

Tyrannosaur. A brown bear skull is broader and stubbier, with shorter, blunter teeth better suited for grinding up the vegetable matter that forms the bulk of its diet.

At the Eskimo Museum, the bus lurches to a stop, and we all march inside. Busloads of foreigners arrive at the museum on an almost hourly basis at this time of year, and the Inuit girl who leads us through the museum is as smooth as a car dealer. Widely regarded as the best place in the Canadian north to see exhibits that demonstrate how the Inuit survived in the Arctic, the Eskimo Museum is run by the local Roman Catholic diocese. It might seem odd that a church would operate a museum, but the early missionaries were serious students of the Inuit way of life. They travelled by dog team, lived in snow houses, ate raw seal meat and learned the language. In 1944 a group of missionaries collected their writings, photographs and Inuit artefacts in the bishop's residence in Churchill, and that facility now contains thousands of items dating back to the prehistoric era. In one corner of the museum, a stuffed polar bear illustrates the monstrous size of the creature they were dealing with.

A fully grown male polar bear is the largest land-dwelling carnivore on the planet. By body weight, it can be three times the size of a Bengal tiger. Standing up on its hind legs, a very large male polar bear is twelve feet tall. The average residential ceiling is eight feet high, so add another four feet and imagine a bear that size looking down at you. In ancient days, polar bears would have made the Arctic coastline a deadly place to live, and exhibits of spears, knives and bows and arrows demonstrate the flimsy-looking weapons the early Inuit had for self-defence. The Inuit sometimes sheltered in snow houses, or "igloos," and these would have been particularly intriguing to prowling bears. Seals hide in similar spaces, in hollowed-out caves under the snow. Scenting its prey, the bear will pussyfoot towards the cave, then rear up and drive its front feet through the crusted snow, trapping the seal and killing it with a bite to the head. In the twenty-four-hour darkness of the Arctic night, an igloo would have been equally tantalizing, with its aromas of seal oil and raw meat and living creatures. Soundlessly approaching, a bear would give no warning until it reared up and smashed through the ceiling.

A common modern-day myth is that aboriginal peoples had a peaceful relationship with bears. But Inuit people competed with polar bears for the same resources and clashed with them regularly. The Inuit were not as powerful or swift as polar bears, but they had a superior brain. With their hands and intelligence, they built weapons that even a skilled craftsman would have a hard time duplicating today, and they enlisted their brother predator, *Canis lupus,* to help fight against the bear. They offered the wolf domestication and a guaranteed annual income, and in return, asked him to pull the sled and guard the camp. The domesticated wolf became a formidable ally for early aboriginals in their war against bears, and without the dog's help, the Arctic would have been uninhabitable. At night a hunter and his family would stake out a dog a hundred yards from camp as a distant early warning system. (They still use this system. Every fish camp along the Hudson Bay coast has a forlorn-looking husky tethered a safe distance from the camp.) It had to be the right sort of dog, fearful enough that it would yelp and howl when it spotted a prowling bear, but not so timid that it would drop to the ground and cringe in silence. The dog's cries would give warning of an approaching bear and give the hunter enough time to jump from bed, grab his weapon, unleash the dogs and go forth to engage the bear. Dogs hate bears and bears hate dogs, a blood feud rooted in the ancient vendetta between bears and wolves. If you watch dogs harassing a bear, there's delight in their expressions. Dogs get paid to harass bears, but they'd do it for free.

While the dogs kept the polar bear occupied, feinting and biting at its back legs, the hunter would move in and take momentary opportunities to stab the bear with his lance. In Rankin Inlet, Nunavut, an Inuit elder named Moses Alyak told me that the techniques for fighting *Nanuq* were taught to him by his grandfather. He said Nanuq is right-handed or left-handed, like a human, and you can tell which paw he is going to hit you with by the way he tilts his head. "You have to stay on your feet when Nanuq attacks," he said. "He will try to knock you down so he can bite your head. He doesn't bite you until you are on the ground, so you have to back away from him, just like you back away from an angry man. When he swings at you, he will tilt his head and show you which paw he is going to swing with. That's when he exposes his side, and that's when you stab him with your lance."

It's hard to believe that a single man could defeat a bear with nothing but a spear and a few dogs for backup. But consider that the Spanish fighting bull, an enormous, muscular beast bred for truculence—the only large animal on earth, in fact, that will attack a human on sight—can be fought and slain by a man armed only with a sword. With the polar bear, the tactics were not very different—patience, timing and knowledge of the animal's fighting habits. The hunter would continually jab at the bear with his lance until loss of blood and exhaustion did their work, then he would plunge his lance into the bear's heart to finish it off. The routine worked so well that a polar bear was no match for an Inuit hunter with dogs, and the bears knew it. The polar bear is often described as the most formidable predator in the Arctic. But even in pre-gunpowder times, most polar bears would run in fear at one whiff of the little creature on two legs.

* * * *

It's hard to know when Europeans first encountered polar bears. The geographer Pliny mentioned them in his descriptions of the nether regions of the globe, and the king of Egypt, Ptolemy II, kept a captive polar bear in his zoo in Alexandria. The Romans trapped wild animals for the entertainment of the mobs, and in A.D. 57 the Roman scribe Calpurnius described polar bears chasing seals around a flooded arena.

It's doubtful that the Romans sailed all the way to the Arctic to capture bears, but they probably didn't have to, because in ancient days the animal's range was much larger than it is today. Feeding on marine mammals like seals and walruses, the bear would have been able to subsist wherever those food sources lived. And in fact, the bear's Latin name, *Ursus maritimus,* suggests that it wasn't originally so much a "polar" bear as an ocean bear. Place names and oral history suggest that in North America, polar bears once ranged as far south as the coast of Maine.

Early Europeans called them "white bears," and like white whales, white stags and white buffalo, they were thought to possess special powers. The Vikings captured polar bear cubs by killing a mother bear, skinning her and laying her pelt on the ice. The cubs would come and lie on her skin, allowing the killers to encircle the youngsters and capture them with nets. They were then kept as valuable trade commodities, each one worth as much as a shipload of firewood. Changing hands as they moved through the marketplace, the cubs invariably ended up as the precious pets of warlords and kings. Early Christian bishops kept polar bears in their palaces, and in 1253 King Henry III kept a live polar bear in the Tower of London.

The journals of Jacques Cartier make reference to polar bears in the Gulf of St. Lawrence (Cartier's men killed one as it was swimming from island to island). The Basque whale fishery no doubt helped support a large population of bears—whale carcasses would have littered the shore from Labrador to the Saguenay—and Champlain mentioned that natives would not go near Anticosti Island because of the "very dangerous white bears" prowling the shores. In Newfoundland, the bears were equally abundant, and early adventurers shot them at every opportunity. Sometimes the bears were killed for fresh meat, which was described as being "as good as young beef." But often, the bears were chased and killed for no other reason than entertainment.

From the perspective of modern times, it may not be entirely fair to condemn these early explorers. The bears were huge and fearsome, and so abundant that it might have been hard to imagine that an entire population could be wiped out. But that's what happened. Over the course of two hundred years, thousands of polar bears were killed along the northeastern shores of North America, and by the early 1800s the bear was obliterated from the Gulf of St. Lawrence. More disturbing, perhaps, is the offhand cruelty that accompanied the killing. The unedited historical record provides a glimpse into the heart of our own species, and the picture is not pretty. One typical account was written by a doctor who set sail from Aberdeen on the Scottish whaling ship *Hercules,* bound for the whaling grounds of Canada. On Monday, August 22, 1831, the doctor was writing in his cabin when one of his shipmates called down the companionway, "Doc, do you want to go after a bear?"

The doctor recalls in his journal,

> I seized my gun and ran on deck. We got into a boat which was lowering away. There were three bears on some ice between us and the land, which was about ten miles off. We pulled among the loose ice to cut off the bears from the land. After pulling hard for about an hour we got between them and the land. We shouted, blew our fog horn, and made every possible noise to drive them towards the sea. They did not proceed very quickly, as they had many lanes of water to swim over. We got pretty close, when we could see their black noses and we could hear them growling and blowing. They all got on a piece of ice in a body. I fired and wounded one of the small ones, however they all took off at a long gallop across the ice and took the water. We pulled after them with all speed. I fired at the old one but missed. They all swam close together. The mother appeared to caress her cubs with her nose. When we approached within about thirty yards of them the mother turned and charged us open mouthed. Candy our harpooner pushed his lance into her neck. She took the lance in her teeth and dived and came up roaring among our oars. She was so near I could have laid my hand on her. She

seized an oar in her teeth and crushed it. I thrust at her with my lance but could not get it entered right at the first push. After this she turned on her side and Milford finished her. She dropped her head into the water, her last look being directed at her cubs, who were blowing out and swimming out to sea. Robert Crumbie shot one of the young ones with a bullet. The other kept swimming around his dead brother. Milford threw a noose over the other's head and drew him up to the boat's bow, where he hung roaring and biting the boat's stem. He was strangled before reaching the ship. We towed the whole three to the ship and hoisted them on deck. The mother was rather small, only measuring eight feet seven inches in length and three feet high on the fore shoulder. The young ones were nearly as large as their mother, being six feet in length. They were very fat. Their stomachs were full of whale oil. The moon rose over the West Land to-night. The air very calm and serene.

Thanks to this kind of casual brutality, the polar bear's range has shrunk along with its population, and nowadays only about twenty thousand inhabit the northern hemisphere, with about 60 per cent of that population living inside Canada. (There are none in Antarctica, despite those Coca-Cola commercials that depict polar bears dancing with penguins.) Most of Canada's bears live north of the sixtieth parallel, where ten-month winters and bitter cold allow the bear some solitude. Most species of bears have an inverse relationship with people—the more humans, the fewer bears. But the town of Churchill is a kind of open-air laboratory for testing a new sort of relationship between the two species. Not very long ago, perhaps fifty years ago, the world's total population of polar bears had dwindled to five thousand, and only a handful lived around Churchill. During the 1950s, the town was an important refuelling stop for the Strategic Air Command, and the military maintained a forward listening post here to spy on Russian radio communications. There were about ten thousand military servicemen living in Churchill, and many owned guns. Liberal wildlife laws allowed them to shoot any bear they considered threatening, and a polar bear can present a convincing threat just by walking towards someone. Any polar bears that wandered into town were shot on sight by residents, wildlife officers or the RCMP, so in the first half of the twentieth century, the town of Churchill was about the last place you'd want to find yourself if you were one of western Hudson Bay's polar bears.

That began to change in the 1960s, when television sets became ubiquitous, and every Sunday evening, right around dinnertime, programs like *Mutual of Omaha's Wild Kingdom* and *Walt Disney Presents* piped animal stories into North American living rooms. The children of the postwar era were coming of age, and their attitudes about everything from wild creatures to sex were different from their parents'. They were shaped by many incidents and forces—the civil rights movement, popular music, marijuana, The Pill, and so on, but arguably, the most important incident took place before any of them were born—on August 6, 1945, when a USAF Stratofortress called *Enola Gay* opened its bomb-bay doors and dropped a nuclear weapon on Hiroshima. It wasn't so much the resulting death toll (100,000) or the ethics of the bombing (the victims were mostly civilians), but the haunting photograph of that beautiful, apocalyptic cloud rising sixty thousand feet into the upper atmosphere that changed forever the way that educated middle-class kids looked at the world. The bomb was an evolutionary turning point analogous to the scene in *2001: A Space Odyssey*, when the ape learns to use a thigh bone as a weapon. Prior to the bomb, nature was usually cast as the implacable foe, and humanity the stalwart hero. Throughout the centuries of pioneering naval exploration, the mapping of the Arctic seas, the taming of the west, the natural world was the great overpowering force that always defeated mankind's puny enterprises. But the tables turned with the invention of the bomb. Humanity was now omnipotent. The principal scientist involved in this ideological turning point was J. Robert Oppenheimer, the so-called "Father of the Atom Bomb," and he best summed it up. When he stood in that bunker in Los Alamos, New Mexico, and watched that first weapon light up the skies with a flash brighter than a thousand suns, some of his fellow scientists laughed, some fell silent and some wept. Oppenheimer just gazed at that rising mushroom cloud and murmured a phrase from the *Bhagavad-Gita:* "Now I am become Death, the destroyer of worlds."

The shift in public attitudes towards the natural world manifested itself in countless ways. In literature and film, it spawned the anti-hero, the outcast who has no values, no religion and no hope for the future. (In *The Wild One,* a landmark picture released in 1953, a girl asks the motorcycle vagabond played by Marlon Brando what he's rebelling against. He shrugs. "What have you got?") In society, it spawned the hippies and the back-to-the-land movement, which in turn created a whole new wave of interest in native peoples and the environment. With the roles reversed, nature was no longer the enemy but a source of healing and inspiration. Wild animals and wild places became popular subject matter for television shows and quality magazines. And stalwart nature photographers began sallying off into the world's remaining wilderness areas to document the wild creatures before they disappeared. Bears, lions, elephants and other big, dangerous animals were once valued mostly as targets for wealthy big-game hunters. But now a new industry was stirring, and it was called "ecotourism." A whole new generation of affluent nature enthusiasts was eager to pay big dollars, not to shoot dangerous animals but to study them and take reverent photographs.

There was some potential here for Churchill to make a few bucks from its bears—they were right outside town. But there was no easy way to get close to them. In Africa, outfitters were taking tourists out in open vehicles from which they could safely photograph wild animals. But in Churchill, or in any other community in the north, there was a major impediment to launching a photo-safari industry: permafrost.

Without getting too technical, it might be worth a moment or two to explore the conditions that create permafrost, which is the essential condition of the polar bear's terrestrial environment. Atop the planet, there's a cap of cold air shaped like a beanie, which shrinks in the summer and enlarges in the winter. The lower rim of the beanie has uneven edges, scallop-shaped waves that run a thousand miles from crest to crest. The frost line—or, as scientists call it, the "line of continuous permafrost"—corresponds to that scalloped border. If you had the advantage of looking down at North America from space, you'd see that this cap of Arctic air sits atop Canada at a jaunty angle, tugged down on the right side. Similarly, the line of permafrost runs from the northwest down into the southeast. This line of the "true north" cuts right through Churchill, and the permafrost makes everyday activities difficult. The ground is permanently frozen, so anyone who wants to construct a building, dig a hole or even go for a cruise in an off-road vehicle has to cope with it. One might think that frozen ground would make for an ideal travel surface. But when the thin pelt of vegetation is disturbed, the heat of the sun gets in and melts the soil beneath. A building's foundation acts as a heat magnet, gradually sinking into the ground and taking the building with it. A bulldozer can produce a scar in the tundra that lasts for centuries. And a simple Jeep trail can take years to erase. Construction experts have learned how to put up buildings in the north by using thick beds of insulating gravel, but in the 1960s, no one had yet figured out how to drive vehicles on permafrost without causing long-term damage.

In the early 1970s the editors of *National Geographic* magazine decided it was time to start working on a feature article about polar bears. The problem with this story, as with many others dealing with remote areas, would be getting quality original photos. Polar bears and other big predators are difficult to approach, and the story would require serious money for travel, accommodation and local guides. Long periods of time would undoubtedly be spent fruitlessly prowling the landscape and dealing with inevitable turns of bad luck and hostile weather. The polar bear is circumpolar, but most of the regions it inhabits are so inhospitable that any journalistic team would have to mount an expedition along the lines of an assault on the Himalayas. In the course of their preliminary research, the magazine editors made an interesting discovery—there was a good population of polar bears in northern Manitoba, and some of those bears were within striking distance of Churchill. But how would they get out on the land to see them?

When the *National Geographic* team got to Churchill, they checked into a motel and rented a car. There were only a few miles of gravel road around the town, and most of the bears congregated at the dump—not the best setting for shooting the regal nomad of the north. While roaming around the gravel roads and talking to the locals, they heard about a guy who possibly had a solution to their problem. His name was Len Smith, and he worked for the town as a diesel mechanic. Like many backwoods people, Smith was a jack of many trades. He had travelled to Churchill in 1966 to take on a short-term posting with the town's public works department, but he fell in love with the north and stayed. Smith enjoyed tinkering with heavy equipment, and was never as happy as when he was crawling around under a bulldozer. With a shop full of spare parts, tracks, bogey wheels and drive shafts, he amused himself by inventing oddball vehicles. He was especially interested in building something that would travel over the tundra without tearing it up. "I had no business application in mind," he says. "I just thought it would be fun to have a vehicle for roaming around on the tundra."

He mounted a large van body atop a high-clearance chassis, wove in parts from a snowplow and a front-end loader, and mounted the whole contraption on "mud tires"—enormous, low-pressure agricultural tires used on crop sprayers. The resulting vehicle looked like the mutant offspring of a school bus and a monster truck. The cab was ten feet off the ground—high enough to keep the operator safe from polar bears—and the interior was fitted with bunks and a toilet. "It was like the northern version of a camper van," he says. "The *National Geographic* guys had been driving around in a rental car, but when they heard about my tundra buggy they thought it might be just the ticket for getting out there and photographing the bears close up. So I agreed to take them out."

They went out and lived in the contraption for a week. The bears were terrified when they first saw the machine coming. "They ran like hell," says Smith. "The military had been out there doing exercises for years, and they'd been killing the bears. I don't know why they shot them. That was just the way it was in those days. Guys would shoot a bear just so they could sit in the Legion and say, 'I shot a polar bear.' So the bears were very shy of vehicles. But they settled down after a while. We'd park up on a hill and eventually they'd get curious and wander over to us."

They camped in the van, ate frozen sandwiches and slept on the cold metal floor. During the night, the bears rocked the walls of the alien machine, trying to tip it over. The tundra buggy broke down several times during their week-long safari, which presented them with two unappealing choices—stay in the buggy and freeze to death, or set off on the long hike back to Churchill and take their chances with the bears. But Smith managed to go outside and make the repairs when there were no bears around, or when it looked like there were no bears around. "One time, I climbed down and went around to the back, and there was a bear curled up asleep by the back wheel," he says. "He jumped up and took off running, and I jumped back in the machine. I don't know who was more scared, him or me."

Another time they ran out of gas, and the bears wouldn't go away, so he threw a ball of lard as far as he could, and while the bears galloped off to investigate, he jumped down to fill the gas tank. (Haste was essential, as bears can run thirty-five miles per hour.) But with all these minor problems, they managed to get nose-to-nose with the bears and get some extraordinary photographs. "They were roaming all around us like cattle, some of them sleeping, others wrestling. At times we'd have two dozen bears around the vehicle. Sometimes the big boys would stand up and spar like boxers. Just one slap from one of those big paws would kill a human, but they didn't seem to hurt each other. They'd knock each other around for a while, then get overheated and lie down for a nap."

The more time Smith spent with the bears, the more he became comfortable with them. "In those days, you didn't think twice about feeding wildlife," he says. "So we would put out sardines to bring the bears in close for a photograph. After a while, I got pretty confident with them. There was a hatch on top of the vehicle, and I would stand up there, feeding the bears by hand, giving them strips of bacon. They'd stand up and lay both front paws on either side of the hatch and look me right in the face. They could have bitten my head and hauled me out of the vehicle, but they were very polite. They'd take the bacon out of my hand as gentle as can be."

Smith says he became particularly friendly with two bears that always hung around together, a male and a female he named Ozzie and Harriet. "Ozzie was nine feet tall," he says. "He would stand up and lay his paws on the roof, and I'd give him a sardine, then I'd rub him behind the head with a broom. He loved getting scratched by that broom. Sometimes he'd grab the broom handle in his teeth and we'd play tug of war, then he'd pull it away from me and drop it on the ground. After a while, he'd get bored and walk away, and I'd climb down and get the broom. As soon as he saw that I was back in the hatch with the broom, he'd come back for another rubdown. Pretty soon it became like a game, and Ozzie figured out the rules. He'd throw the broom on the ground, walk far enough away that it was safe for me to get out, then as soon as I climbed back into the vehicle, he'd come back for another rubdown."

The journalists went back to their magazine with great photographs, and Smith realized the tundra buggy had business potential. "I could see that wildlife photographers would hire me to take them out, but I never thought the average tourist would be interested. Then I got this group of twenty people who just wanted to look at bears. I had only five miles of trail, and I thought they'd be bored stiff, driving up and down the same trail all week looking at bears, but they just loved it. Then other magazines started running stories about the bears and the tundra buggy, and that attracted more public interest. The phone started ringing, and before you know it there were hundreds of people coming—tourists from all over the world. We'd put them up in the hotels and feed them in groups at the restaurants. I was building new tundra buggies as fast as I could, just to stay ahead of the demand. I never thought it would turn into the enormous thing that it did, but people just love to watch these bears. And it wasn't boring for me because I love watching the bears too. They are very, very intelligent animals and they're always doing something new. I watched bears for twenty years and I never got tired of it. Every single day was fascinating."

Smith sold his company in 1999 and retired to Florida, where he now has a nice life, soaking up the sun and fishing in his own boat on the Gulf of Mexico. But he says his misses the north, and the bears. In 2006 the provincial government awarded him the Order of Manitoba for his pioneering work in founding the bear-watching industry that now brings millions of dollars into Churchill. There are now a dozen buggies going out on the tundra every day, and for most tourists, a tundra buggy tour is pretty much mandatory, like going to Niagara Falls and booking a ride on the *Maid of the Mist*.

We were scheduled to get out on the buggies the day after we arrived, so after checking into our motel, going for dinner and getting a good night's sleep, we rose about an hour before dawn, looking forward to hitting the tundra and seeing some bears. One of the rewards of a small group tour like this is getting to know people from other places, and during breakfast, I was pleased to take a seat with some of my new chums, including a retired judge from Utah named Robert Braithwaite, who was travelling the world with his young daughter Hope.

Robert is typical of the intelligent, well-read class of traveller that you meet on these eco-tours. He thinks that wild animals and wild places are under siege, but he's not tedious about it. He's curious and wants to learn about polar bears and what can be done to preserve the species. He says that as an American he feels some responsibility for what he describes as "this mess we're in." And when we first met, he made a jocular point of informing me that even though he is from Utah, he doesn't think the Rapture is coming and doesn't have three wives back home. Hope, his eleven-year-old daughter, is angelic and noble, in the way that young, well-behaved girls are just before they start turning into teenagers. She and her dad take these trips regularly, going to different parts of North America and seeing face to face what the environmental issues are. Hope writes everything in her journal and presents those accounts to her classmates when she gets home. Robert says he wants to travel with her now, before she attains adolescence and doesn't like him anymore, but he's a kidder, and it's Hope's job to roll her eyes and play the straight man to her dad's comic patter. When I first met him, he said,

"Hi, my name's Robert and this is my daughter Hope. We're Bob and Hope." As we finish our breakfast, Hope studies a brochure about the tundra buggies. She is fascinated by bears, especially polar bears. She draws them and writes stories about them, even though she has never seen one. And when I tell her I saw bear tracks right behind the motel, she only smiles, accustomed to adults pulling her leg.

Being a retired judge, Robert probably has a bit of money in the bank, but not everyone on the tour is affluent. While we're eating breakfast, we're joined by another couple, two schoolteachers from northern England. Alan, the husband, is a birdwatcher, and yesterday, when we were trundling around town in the tour bus, he ignored our guide's narrative and spent the whole time staring out the window, scanning the frozen tundra. "He's hoping to see a snowy owl," his wife explains in a low voice as Alan goes to fetch her a coffee. "It's his number one dream for this trip. I really hope he sees one. We saved for three years so he can see a snowy owl."

Daylight is blanching the eastern horizon, and after breakfast we get dressed in heavy boots and parkas, pack up our cameras and daypacks and troop outside to climb on our bus, a lime-green antique that looks like *Furthur*, the bus Neal Cassady drove for Ken Kesey. Our driver, Sheldon Olivier, is a smart, straight-talking wilderness guide with a shaved head and goatee who has lived in Churchill for more than ten years. I grab a seat behind him, and as we bounce out of the lot and head south, he tells me his girl-friend owns our motel. He lives outside town in a weathered cabin where roaming polar bears are common. He says it's like living on the same street as a gang clubhouse—the bears make it an inter-esting neighbourhood, but they hold the real estate values down.

"You have to keep your eyes open when you leave the house in the morning," he says. "Nature has designed them for pure silence. And because they're white, there could be one lying in the snow just a few yards away. One minute, you think you're all alone; the next minute, there's a bear right in front of you. They just appear out of nowhere."

When I tell him I saw bear tracks behind the motel, he says it's not uncommon. He's seen them walking right through the middle of town. And although they saunter along slowly, they can burst into life in an instant. "They go from a slow walk to a sprint just like that," he says, snapping his fingers. "And you have to stay on your toes, because you never know when you're going to meet one. Right now the kids are going to school, and there are trucks and people all over the place, but there could be a polar bear walking down that back lane. You can tell someone who lives in Churchill because they never step outside without taking a look."

Like a lot of Churchill people, Sheldon takes pride in the local campaign of peaceful coexistence with the bears. But the relationship is founded on *realpolitik*, and even the most devoted photographers, biologists and nature guides tend to pack firearms for insurance. Sheldon keeps a heavy rifle—a Holland & Holland .375—racked above the driver's seat, and though he says it's unlikely he'll ever have to use it, he likes to know it's there in case someone gets jumped by a bear. As we roll through town, an elderly lady in our group asks Sheldon if he's ever had to shoot a bear. Sheldon nods, as though he's been expecting this question. "In all the years I've lived in Churchill, I've only had to destroy one bear, and that was two weeks ago. This one particular bear was causing a lot of problems out where I live. One night, I heard a big ruckus, and a minute later the bear was coming through my front door with two big angry dogs attached to his rear end. I shot him right there in the entrance. I thought the wildlife officers would give me a hard time, but they were really fed up with this animal, and they agreed that I didn't have any choice."

The tundra buggies deploy from a launch site a few miles out of town, and they're all lined up at their piers. More than four hundred people take these tundra buggy tours every day, seven days a week. You walk down a plywood concourse and gather at your plywood departure gate. It's like being in an airport, except it's twenty below zero inside the terminal. We have no sooner bounced out of the parking lot than the buggy heaves to a stop beside a snoozing polar bear. Grabbing our cameras, we all hasten outside onto the viewing platform, which is a railed pulpit about ten feet off the ground. The bear is curled up in the lee of a willow clump with eyes half closed, waiting disconsolately for the arrival of winter.

The bear knows we're looking down at him but doesn't seem to care. Hope Braithwaite, bundled up in her parka, is staring down at the bear. I catch her eye, but she doesn't want to talk. She leans against the rail, gazing at the drowsing bear, and writes a line in her notebook: *It's beautiful.*

Our guide tells us that hundreds of bears gather here every autumn, waiting for Hudson Bay to freeze so they can go out on the ice and hunt ringed seals. The Churchill area has the world's southernmost population of polar bears. Unlike most of their species, they've developed a unique feast-and-famine survival strategy, fasting all summer and eating ringed seals all winter. According to our tour guide, the bears don't bother to eat the skin of a seal. After eating the fat, they leave the leftover on the ice—a hollowed-out bag of skin that looks like a collapsed potato. The buffet really kicks into gear in the late winter and spring, when the seal pups are born. The pups are about 50 per cent fat and they aren't wary, so the bears can really pack on a lot of weight in the last few weeks of the hunting season. If there is an unseasonably early thaw, it can be hard on the seal population, because the rain melts their snow caves and the pups are exposed on the bare ice, making them easy pickings for foxes and bears. If the ice goes out early, it can be hard on the bears too, because their feeding binge is curtailed. Each day of feeding is doubly detrimental—the fasting period is longer, and the bears go into the fast with less stored body fat.

Dr. Ian Stirling has used NASA satellite photos to track the historic arrival of spring, and has found that the breakup of sea ice is coming about a week earlier with each decade. An extra week of fasting can have a serious impact on a polar bear, and Stirling also determined that the average weight of polar bears in the western Hudson Bay population is declining.

There are nineteen recognized populations of polar bears in the world. Those around Churchill belong to the so-called "western Hudson Bay population," which consists of about a thousand animals. The nineteen recognized populations are not distinct enough to be considered subspecies, but they stick to well-defined areas, interbreed and practise skills and cultural behaviours specific to that region. Each bear survives in its own region courtesy of knowledge passed down to it by its mother. In 1980 the average female in the Churchill area weighed 650 pounds. Recently, the average weight of these bears has dropped to 507 pounds, a loss of almost 150 pounds. Very thin female polar bears weighing less than about 420 pounds don't come into season and don't become pregnant—for the obvious reason that they won't be able to provide enough milk and the cubs won't survive. If spring continues to come earlier—and that seems to be the trend—the bears in the Churchill area will continue to lose body weight, and at some point in the near future (in thirty or forty years, according to Stirling), the females will cease bearing young, and the Churchill population of bears, the southernmost group of polar bears, will die off.

The tundra buggy kicks into motion, and we go looking for more bears. It's a sunny morning, and the landscape looks like a frozen sea. Distant buggies are inching back and forth on the horizon like prowling bugs. It would be interesting to stand on the observation platform as we bounce along, but even with heavy parkas and facial scarves, the wind is as sharp as sheet metal. Every fifteen minutes or so, the buggy stops as someone spots a fox, an Arctic hare or a group of white ptarmigan amongst a distant clutch of willows. Everyone keeps changing camera lenses and scrambling for different filters. Our group has brought along so many massive cameras it's like being caught up with a group of excited parents at a kindergarten performance. Soon enough, we arrive at a windswept point next to the purple waters of the bay. About a dozen bears are lying in the snow or sauntering about, their fur rippling in the sharp wind. Some of the bears are uncomfortably hot—as hard as that is to believe—and have dug holes down to the frost layer to make a pleasant bed of frozen black mud. One big male has excavated a bed with a large stone for a built-in pillow. Stretched out on his chest, his chin resting on the stone, he watches us with flat boredom.

Our driver tells me that the early tundra buggies were only about eight feet high, with a roof hatch and open windows to allow photographers to shoot bears close up. As it turned out, eight feet wasn't high enough. One photographer, in fact, had a nasty surprise when a bear came out from under the machine and grabbed his arm. "It was a very large, skinny male," the driver tells me. "The photographer stuck the whole camera out the window so he could focus the telephoto lens on a bird. This big, old, skinny male bear was under the buggy. He stood up and grabbed the photographer by the arm. He just caught the skin on the bottom of the arm, and that was lucky, or he would have torn the man's arm off."

Modern tundra buggies have viewing platforms more than ten feet off the ground and closed-in skirting all around. But still, experienced photographers keep their eyes open, always shoulder-checking for a bear that might slip from an unexpected direction and pull a fast move of some kind. Rumours persist of super-bears, two-thousand-pounders that can stand thirteen feet on their back legs—tall enough to pluck someone off the viewing platform. This might sound like the usual hyperbole. But one seasoned-looking photographer tells me that a few years ago, he went outside on the platform with another photographer to take a pict ure of a snowy owl. He was changing lenses when he felt a tug on his parka. The other photographer yanked him away. A huge bear was looking at them over the railing, with a scrap of fabric in its teeth. "So you have to be careful," he warns me. "Don't let your arms droop over the rail, and don't let their sleepy demeanour fool you."

One of the tour companies has built a "tundra buggy hotel" here by linking together a group of the vehicles. You can stay here for a couple of days and spend the whole time watching bears. From anyplace in the world, anytime during bear season, you can also log on to the Internet and watch live video from the "polar bear cam" mounted on the wall of the tundra buggy hotel.

Just as people around the world watch the bears, so too do the bears watch the humans. Periodically, one of the bears prowling around the tundra buggy hotel rears up on its hind legs and gazes into the lens of the video camera. An instant later, a zoomed-in image of the bear's face appears on a computer screen in someone's home office in Malibu or Turin.

Our own driver is a young man from Australia, with a beard and a globetrotter's zest for wildlife and wild places. He tells us that he'll do this job for a while and then move on to his next adventure. He says that once in a while a bear will approach this vehicle, throw its paws against the hood and stare at him through the windshield. He adds that he once had a bear climb up onto the front tire and open the door handle with its teeth. "It was one smooth motion," he says. "This guy was smarter than the average bear." As the door swung open, he tried to hit the bear's nose with a thermos bottle. "He kept pulling his nose back. They're very fast. I'd slam the door, and he'd open it again. I punched the gas and got the hell out of there. Then I got on the radio: 'Hey, be careful, you guys, we have a bear that knows how to open doors.'"

Throughout the day we see dozens of bears, white foxes, Arctic hares and some of the scurrying white ptarmigan that are the northern equivalent of the prairie grouse. There are over two hundred species of birds nesting in the Churchill area, and the gradually warming climate will no doubt affect them as well. As we go grinding and bouncing back to the terminal in the fading light of late afternoon, I listen to the different conversations going on in the big tundra buggy. There's a Japanese couple in the back seat, speaking in their own language, and a couple of Germans in the next seat, talking away in theirs. A documentary film producer from Paris and her husband are in the front of the bus, talking to the biologist from California about her polar bear skull, and Bob and Hope from Utah are sitting across the aisle from me. All these people have come to Churchill, and you can't help but wonder what they're gaining from the experience. I ask Hope why she has come all this way to look at bears. She thinks about it for a moment. "Because they're an endangered species," she says. "And they're kind of scary."

The bears *are* endangered, *and* they're kind of scary. It seems like a contradiction, but it pretty much defines our essential fascination with the polar bear. We human beings know how to fly. We've walked on the moon. We can destroy cities with the click of a mouse, but something inside us still wants to believe that nature is both more delicate and more powerful than us. Like Melville's white whale, the polar bear is the great blankness upon which we project our fears and intrigues. Churchill is one big bazaar of bear memorabilia—plush toys, polar bear T-shirts, polar bear coffee mugs—and while most of those images depict polar bears as fluffy and amiable, it's the animal's reputation as the terrestrial world's largest meat-eating predator that really fascinates the tourists. We seem to love the bear because it's one of the few animals in the world that still regards us as potential food.

Don't Walk
in This Area

In the last thirty years, polar bears have killed seven people in Canada, and some of those were in Churchill. In one case, two native kids tracked a polar bear through the fresh snow, and when they caught up to it the bear killed one of them. In 1986, a homeless man was rummaging through the remains of a burned-out hotel in downtown Churchill, stuffing frozen hamburger patties in his pockets, when a bear came up from behind, grabbed him, then started dragging him down the street. People saw what was happening and raised the alarm. Somebody ran up to a house and hammered on the door. "A bear is killing a man! We need a gun!"

Andrew Lee told me the story. He and I were sitting in the bar in the Seaport Hotel having a beer when I asked him about the attack. "Who killed the bear?"

"Me."

Andrew was twenty-one years old when I interviewed him, a businesslike young man with wet-combed hair like Clark Kent. He was scrupulously polite in that sort of steady-eyed manner that some northerners have. As he began telling me the story of the bear attack, an intoxicated and tough-looking Chipewyan man came over and asked him for five dollars. Andrew ignored him. The man came back a few minutes later and interrupted Andrew again, this time pulling at his jacket. Andrew became mildly vexed. "Excuse me," he said. He stood up, seized the man by the lapels, punched him once in the head and threw his limp body under the pool table. "Sorry about that," he said, pulling up his chair and continuing his story.

"I was watching the hockey game when I heard shouting outside," he said. "Then somebody banged on the door and yelled, 'A bear is killing a man!' I grabbed a shotgun, put on my gumboots and ran outside, thumbing slugs into the gun as I ran down the street in my underwear. I saw the bear crouched over a guy on the front street, biting him. I ran up and hoofed the bear in the rear end, as hard as I could, but it had no effect. So I put the muzzle against his chest and let him have it."*

More recently there was a gruesome attack on some Inuit people at Corbett Inlet, along the Hudson Bay coastline. I heard

---

* Later on that year, Andrew was driving a Caterpillar train to Arviat when his tractor plunged through the sea ice, taking him to the bottom of Hudson Bay. Like a lot of backwoods Canadian communities, Churchill is not a good place to live if you work in the outdoors and hope to grow old. Of the five people I became acquainted with during that visit, three were killed in various accidents before the year was out.

that story in 2001, and finally met one of the main characters, sixty-six-year-old Moses Aliyak. Moses is a pale-skinned, rather Caucasian-looking Inuk with the stately, lined face of an aged Henry Fonda. I met him at a tent camp north of Rankin Inlet, Nunavut. He and his relatives were catching char and drying them on racks in the sun. A rusty .22 rifle was on the bed in his tent and there were tins of beans, bully beef and Carnation evaporated milk on the wooden slats that served as shelving. Sitting on plastic crates outside his tent, we drank tea while he told me, through a translator, about what happened that day. He prefaced the story by saying that he has been attacked by polar bears three times, and the third time was the worst. He wears a wool cap to cover his head, but he took it off to show me the claw marks— deep furrows across the bare dome of his skull.

Moses said he was only slightly injured in the first two incidents. The first time he was attacked it was snowing and he was wearing white, and a female Nanuq charged him, thinking he was another bear. She swatted him once, realized he was a man and ran away. The second time, he was at Whale Cove. He went scouting and left his ten-year-old grandson Kook to mind the cabin. While he was away, Kook looked outside the cabin and saw some bears coming. He climbed up on the roof, shouting for help. The bears went inside the cabin while Kook scrambled around the roof, frantic with fear that the bears would climb up on the roof and get him after they were finished looting the cabin. Moses came walking over the hill and saw Kook on the roof. Then a big Nanuq came out the door of the cabin, followed by two cubs. The mother bear saw Moses and ran up the hill to attack him. He backed away from her, trying to keep his feet, but she hit him hard with a right hook and tore his arm open. "I didn't want the bear to kill me," he explained, "because I didn't want Kook to see that." After hitting him, the mother bear took her cubs and ran off.

The final time, he was attacked by a full-grown cub. He suspected it was a third cub of the litter, and explained that third cubs are particularly dangerous. He said a mother Nanuq doesn't have cubs every year. She needs to gather her strength and build up her fat supply so she can make enough milk to feed them. Every couple of years, when she is fat enough, she will become pregnant. She will come off the sea when the ice breaks up in June. All summer she will do very little, digging shallow depressions in the earth and lying on the permafrost to stay cool. In the fall, when the other bears go back out on the ice, she will dig a den in the soft earth of a side hill. She will give birth to her cubs during one of the long nights in December. In her whole lifetime, if she is lucky and healthy, she will give birth four or five times, and most of those times she will only give birth to two cubs. But one winter, if she is in very fine condition, she might give birth to three. Born blind and toothless, the cubs are only the size of a woman's foot. But they are covered with short, smooth fur and they stay warm by nestling against her and drinking her milk, which is very rich, like cream, and smells like seal oil. In April she opens the den and takes the cubs outside. They are as big as small dogs now, but they are still too weak and dim-witted to travel. The mother relaxes outside, lying on her back in the snow and enjoying the spring sunshine. While the cubs nurse, she rocks them in her arms and makes humming noises, just like a human mother.

Moses said that after several weeks the cubs are ready to take a trip out onto the sea ice to hunt for seals. On the journey to the sea ice, the cubs chase each other, wrestling in the snow. It looks like harmless play but they are learning how to fight and kill, and they are learning which one is dominant. Often, the third cub, the extra one, cannot compete with his first-born brother and sister. They are bigger and more assertive, and they take most of the mother's milk for themselves. When mother and cubs arrive on the sea ice, she teaches them how to hunt. She can smell a seal from a mile away. She shows them how to study the ice and creep close enough to the seal to grab it before it can escape down its breathing hole. Again, the stronger cubs take the best food for themselves. The cubs stay with their mother for three years. When they are almost fully grown, she sends them away. In times of plentiful food the runty third cub might survive, but even then, in Moses's opinion, he will continue to resent the way he was abused by his siblings. Moses said that a fully grown third cub is the most dangerous animal in the Arctic.

On July 9, 1999, Moses and his grandson Kook, who was then twelve years old, and some other people went to visit the place where Moses grew up, Corbett Inlet. They set up a camp there, and while they were in their tents the tide came up and the boat drifted away, with Moses's gun in it. A woman named Margaret said she'd swim out and get the boat, but he said, "No, don't do that. You'll get hypothermia." Margaret went to a nearby freshwater spring to fill their canteen. The others went into a tent and made tea, and Moses called Baker Lake on the radio and told them they'd lost their boat. Then Moses and Kook went outside. As soon as Moses stepped out of the tent, he saw movement and froze. Right next to the tent, right between the tent and the guy ropes, was Nanuq.

The bear sprang towards him. Moses ran, trying to make the bear chase him instead of Kook. As he ran, he tried to get the knife on his belt, but he'd left the knife inside the tent. Nanuq chased him and wrapped its arms around him, tackling him to the ground. Kook was yelling at the bear, trying to scare it away from his grandfather, but Moses shouted, "Run away or he'll attack you!" The bear was chewing at the back of his neck, trying to bite his spine and paralyze him, but Moses had his hands clamped over the back of his neck and the bear couldn't get a good grip. For several minutes the bear kept biting through his hands, trying to crack his spine. Moses wouldn't move his hands. Finally, the bear got frustrated. Moses rose from his seat on the plastic milk crate to impersonate the bear, woofed and shook his head, and showed me how the animal angrily held him down with one foot and clawed at him with the other, tearing off his scalp.

That's when Moses's friend Hattie Amitnak, sixty-six, and her ten-year-old grandson Eddie Amitnak came running up to help. The bear whirled around and chased them. Moses couldn't see because of the blood in his eyes. The bear struck Eddie and knocked him down. Then it attacked Hattie. Moses could hear her screaming as the bear dragged her away. He heard ripping sounds as the bear began eating Hattie, then he passed out.

Margaret Amarook came walking back from the spring, carrying the canteen of fresh water. She wondered what was wrong because everything seemed so quiet in the camp. Then she saw the polar bear by the tent. It raised its head and looked at her. It was eating Hattie, and had blood on its face. Margaret ran up to Moses, who was lying on the ground with his scalp torn off. Moses couldn't see, and he told her, "I think the bear is devouring my grandson."

Margaret called out for Kook, and he answered from inside the tent. "I'm scared!" Kook shouted. "There's a polar bear near us. Don't go near us!"

Eddie had likewise escaped from the bear. Margaret told Moses she would run and get help from David and Rosie Oolooyuk, who were camped out two miles away. They had a single-sideband radio and could call the RCMP. Margaret set off for the other camp and was halfway there when she saw Moses staggering after her. She helped him, but he fell down many times. When they reached the Oolooyuks' cabin, people there splashed water on his wounds. Moses wouldn't enter the cabin because he was soaked in blood and didn't want to terrify the children who were cowering inside. Moses told them that the bear would follow the blood trail and smash down the door to get him. "Leave me outside," he said. "And block the door so Nanuq can't get in."

They radioed for help, and soon two helicopters arrived, one loaded with nurses and RCMP officers, the other with wild-life officers who went off in search of the bear. They found it three miles away from the camp and shot it. The bear was two and a half years old, and was probably a third cub. Moses went to Winnipeg, where he was treated for his injuries. Kook went along to take care of him.

Moses's insistence on staying outside the cabin when he knew the bear would come after him was seen by everyone as an act of great courage, and a year later he was nominated for a Medal of Bravery. He was supposed to fly to Ottawa to attend a formal ceremony at Rideau Hall and receive his medal from Governor General Adrienne Clarkson. But he couldn't make it because Rankin Inlet had one of its typical whiteouts and his airplane was grounded.

No one has been killed by a bear in the western Hudson Bay region since that incident at Corbett Inlet in 1999. There are more bears around Churchill than ever, but few attacks, and that's entirely because the townspeople have become so good at coexisting with the big animals. There's an emergency hotline for bear problems (675-BEAR), and signs warn of traditional bear paths—DON'T WALK IN THIS AREA. Most of the town's stores and restaurants give their employees rides home after dark, and if you're attending a function or taking a late meal in a downtown restaurant, the locals get concerned if you tell them you're walking back to your motel by yourself. This takes a little getting used to, given that Churchill is a modern-looking community, with lots of restaurants, a supermarket, a Home Hardware and spacious suburbs with split-level homes and condo complexes. It also has back alleys and windswept, snowy railyards from which a roaming polar bear might appear at a moment's notice. So if you're walking anywhere in town after dark, you're supposed to take a few steps and look back over your shoulder—it's the Churchill two-step. The townscape is riddled with empty lots and shadows and great, frozen humps of snow, so it's not hard for a polar bear to mosey around for a while before anyone notices it. When that happens, the phone rings in the office of Sydney McGregor, the local conservation officer.

That evening, after our tundra buggy tour, I walked down to meet with Sydney McGregor and find out how he helps to keep the peace between bears and people. His office is in the town complex, an immense warren that would be the envy of any affluent community in the south. It contains the local school, public library, swimming pool, curling rink, basketball gym, movie theatre and multiple stores and offices. Sydney McGregor and his fellow game wardens (they are officially called conservation officers) work out of an office there and regularly patrol the town. McGregor, like most conservation officers, is a physi-cally fit, outdoorsy kind of guy who enjoys the unpredictability of the job. "You're doing many jobs rolled into one," he says. "Sometimes you're a cop and sometimes you're a schoolteacher and sometimes you're a trapper. One day you might be slogging across the tundra, and the next day you might be working at a desk all day, so you have to be adaptable."

He came up here because he wanted to work with polar bears. The town is very friendly, and everybody welcomed him. "By your third day here, everyone in town knows your name. It's not a road-rage sort of place. The downside is, everyone knows everyone else's business. As the locals say, 'If you haven't heard a rumour by ten in the morning, start one.'" He says Churchill is a three-year posting, and just about all the wardens in Manitoba want to work here at least once. But it's a round-the-clock job during the ninety-day bear season. The office closes at midnight, but one officer is always on call. McGregor says it's a rare night when a bear doesn't wander into town. "Sometimes I'll be lucky enough to sleep all night. But other nights I might get two or three calls, and it's not always the same bear."

He keeps his boots and equipment ready to go. From the moment the phone rings beside his bed and he steps into his boots and rolls out the door to the place where the bear was sighted, his average response time is three to six minutes. He can track the bear's journey through town by the sound of barking dogs. His pickup truck looks like a police vehicle, with two-tone paint and wigwags on the roof. If the bear doesn't run when it sees him coming, he flashes the lights and blips the siren. The bear heads down the street at a gallop, and he chases it towards the outskirts of town. When it gets to the edge of town, he might jump out of the truck and rack the slide on his shotgun and give it a good send-off. He has different types of ammunition for his shotgun, the most useful being "cracker shells," which arc through the air and explode at the bear's heels with a terrifying bang. "It's for their own good," he says. "The last thing we need is for bears to get the idea they're welcome to come into town and scrounge for food. There's an expression that 'a fed bear is a dead bear,' and the kindest thing we can do is scare the heck out of them."

Sometimes a bear isn't impressed with all his noise and flashing lights. McGregor says you have to be careful getting out of the vehicle around the surly ones. Sometimes a mother bear with COYs (cubs of the year) will come after him and he has to jump into the vehicle. He says Halloween is his most worrisome time of the year. It's the peak of bear season, and the town is crawling with plump little ghosts and goblins carrying sacks of toffee, chocolate and other aromatically intriguing ursine treats. "We take Halloween very, very seriously." A couple of days ahead of time, he goes into classrooms and talks to the kids, telling them the rules. (Nobody is allowed to dress like a seal, for example.) Then he and his fellow wardens meet with the RCMP, the Canadian Rangers, Parks Canada, local volunteers and other groups. At four o'clock on Halloween afternoon, he loads a tranquilizer gun and goes up in a helicopter and flies around the town, checking for bears. On the ground, mobile patrols go out and establish a perimeter. The kids go trick-or-treating in groups, with armed adult volunteers accompanying them and an RCMP patrol car bringing up the rear. At ten o'clock, the air-raid siren on the roof of the town complex goes off, signalling that Halloween is over for another year and the kids have to go home.

"So far, we've managed to run a safe Halloween every year," says McGregor. "And we intend to keep it that way."

All these precautions have paid off, in that the town manages to put a thousand bears and ten thousand people together every autumn without mishap. But still, just about everyone who lives in Churchill has had a close call at one time or another. As a waitress at the local restaurant told me one morning, "When you're new here, you're afraid of the bears, but it's a fear based on ignorance. Then, as you learn more about them, you lose your fear. Then, after you've lived here for a long time, you learn even more about them and you start becoming afraid again. You can tell someone who's lived here for a while because they're always glancing over their shoulder as they walk down the street."

When you take a tundra buggy tour, the guides are always emphasizing the intelligence of the bears, their superb adaptability, their grace and their survival skills. Scaring people with bear stories is considered to be a bit off-message. The tourists pick up on that, and you can see them resisting the urge to ask about hair-raising encounters. But when the tours are over and everyone is roaming around the town on their own, that's when the curiosity comes out. Everyone knows they're supposed to be focusing on the bear as a Marvel of Nature. But when the tourists are shooting the breeze with the bartender or the taxi driver or the lady managing the local trading post, they just want to hear a good story about the time somebody almost got their arm ripped off.

Penny Rawlings hears these questions all the time. She is the governess of the Arctic Trading Company—the premier store in Churchill to shop for Inuit art, furs, moccasins and other mementos of the north—and her shop functions as the town's main hangout. You could stand in the foyer, and sooner or later every tourist in town would walk in. Clad in rough wood and bedecked with caribou antlers and wolf hides, the Arctic Trading Company looks like the sort of northern trading post depicted in old-style television shows like *Sergeant Preston of the Yukon*. Penny and her husband, Keith, started it thirty years ago. Keith was an Englishman, and was cut from the same fabric as the swaggering, hard-nosed Brits who used to manage the entire planet as if it was theirs by primogeniture. When I first met Keith, back in the 1980s, he seemed to have the world by the tail. He styled himself as the governor of the Arctic Trading Company and looked like a character from another era, like an officer of the Bengal Lancers—handlebar mustache, booming jocular voice and a charming impatience with the established method of doing things. Under his governance, the Arctic Trading Company built an international reputation as the north's best source of unique Arctic handicrafts and high-quality soapstone art. He prowled his north in his own airplane, hobnobbed with art collectors from New York and London and acted as an agent for the carvers and artisans from Baker Lake, Frobisher Bay and other Inuit communities. His best asset was his wife, Penny, an attractive, businesslike blonde who kept the business together.

One night, Keith loaded his airplane with freight and passengers, among them Bishop Robidoux of the Oblate Mission, and took off from Rankin Inlet. The plane climbed out, then wing-stalled and crashed. It may or may not have been overloaded, depending on whether you believe that Keith was the type of guy to overload a plane. Everyone died in the burning wreckage. With Keith's death, people assumed that Penny would sell the company and leave Churchill. After all, Keith was the public face of the Arctic Trading Company, and it's rare to see female entre-preneurs in the north. But Penny was determined to carry on the business. Despite resistance and skepticism from bankers, and major debts resulting from the plane crash, she developed a new business plan and worked hard for the next ten years, putting the company back on its feet. Today, the Arctic Trading Company has regained its place in the centre of town, and Penny has earned her title of governess. She is one of the most prominent women in the Canadian north, and has the personal strength and cha-risma of a widow from one of those 1940s Hollywood westerns, running the ranch by herself and waiting for Shane. Her store is one of those quaint places where you could easily while away the afternoon, just soaking up the aroma of woodsmoke and wolf pelts. The shelves are lined with books and carvings, and you don't have to look very hard to find something to do with polar bears. "When people come in here, that's what many of them are looking for," Penny says. "They're looking for something to take home with a polar bear on it."

Some days, the shoppers don't have to sort through the T-shirts and coffee mugs and Eskimo statuary to find a good image of a bear. "We sometimes get real live bears right outside our back door," she says. "We're right in the middle of town, but that doesn't seem to matter. If my employees are working late, I make sure they have a ride home."

A few years ago, some customers came into her store and told her they hadn't been able to find any bears. It was summer-time, and the bears hadn't really migrated into the area yet. But Penny knew a secret spot where you could usually find a bear even in the summertime: the town dump. "They're not very photogenic, all covered with soot," she says. "But at least they're bears." She loaded her guests in her van and took them to the dump. Sure enough, a big male polar bear was rooting in the trash, and her guests were thrilled to take some photos. When it came time to leave, she put the van in reverse and discovered that the wheels had sunk into the soft sand. She rocked it back and forth, but it just sank deeper. "This was a real dilemma," she said. "Some of my guests were big guys who could have easily pushed it out, but there was no way they wanted to get out of the van with that big bear only fifty feet away."

She blew the horn and flashed the lights, trying to scare the bear away. The bear ignored her. She was worried that she would deplete the battery or run out of gas and they would be stuck in the dump all night, surrounded by bears that could easily break the windshield or pull the doors off if they put their minds to it. Finally, after prolonged blaring, the bear wandered off. The men opened the sliding door of the van, climbed out and began rocking it back and forth as Penny revved the engine. She was shouting directions at them when she noticed something in the rear-view mirror. It was like that scene in *Moby Dick*, where a tiny white spot appears in the translucent waters far beneath Ahab's whale boat. The white spot in Penny's mirror grew rapidly in size until it transformed itself into a polar bear coming towards the van at a full gallop. She yelled at her guests, "Get inside!!" They jumped into the van and slammed the door just as the bear arrived. Fortunately, the van was free and they were able to drive away.

Why does one bear behave aggressively and another flee at the sight of humans? The question hints at our need to see bears as simplistic animals, symbols of a natural world that is reliably benign or savage depending on our point of view. As one

Churchill local told me: "You can't predict what a bear will do. If someone starts telling you how a polar bear will act in this or that situation, it's a sign he doesn't know what he's talking about." Scientists and photographers who watch polar bears for years say that some bears are good-natured, while others are timid, playful or downright foul-tempered. Their responses are governed by the same vagaries of nature and nurture that shape the personalities of all higher animals, even *Homo sapiens*. Dr. Ian Stirling of the Canadian Wildlife Service has studied bears for more than thirty years. He has seen a bear stop in its tracks while prowling the sea ice, and spend a minute or two figuring out how to sneak up on a distant seal. One day, he watched a bear calculate an approach to a sleeping seal, then drop onto its belly and slither its way up a shallow meltwater creek towards its prey. The bear came to a fork in the watercourse, bellied a short distance up the wrong one, then carefully shifted into reverse, wriggling backwards on its belly, and took the other. "These animals are consistently surprising," he says. "The more we study them, the more I realize how little we know."

* * * *

When tourists come to Churchill, they spend most of their time in tundra buggies. This is largely because there's no other safe, efficient way of getting large numbers of people into the places where bears live. But the tundra buggy experience isn't for everyone. I have to confess that I've never been a big fan of driving around all day in a bus, even if there are polar bears walking by outside. It's a bit like trundling around in a mobile zoo in which the bears have the run of the place and the visitors are in the cages. It's not the role reversal that's disturbing; it's the creepy feeling that this is a glimpse of the future—a future in which most of the planet will be covered with human habitation, and here and there will be a few no-go zones where wild animals will roam in faux security—observed, of course, by busloads of "ecotourists" like us.

If you want to get off the bus and walk around polar bear country on foot, you have to go with a specialized guide who will take you out to meet bears face to face. Doug Webber runs a polar bear outcamp at a place called Dymond Lake. Doug is the biggest tourist outfitter in Churchill and has been in the business for a long time. He has fishing lodges, hunting camps and ecotourism lodges all over this part of northern Manitoba, and his lodge at Dymond Lake specializes in taking small groups of polar bear enthusiasts on walking safaris into the bear's habitat. I try to visit Doug whenever I am in Churchill, and this particular week, since he is "out on the land," as they say around here, he sends his son-in-law Nelson Morberg down to the airport to pick me up. It's a bright, fiercely cold day, and after Nelson has taken care of a few errands, we go slip-sliding on the icy pavement out to the family airplane, a bright yellow De Havilland Beaver with STOL scoops on the wings and fat tundra tires. The tarmac has been polished to black marble by the wind, and, like most people who live here full time, Nelson is underdressed in a skimpy jacket. Airplanes love cold air, and as soon as we taxi away, Nelson feeds it some gas and we jump aloft.

Climbing to a thousand feet, Nelson levels off and we cruise over Churchill, the roofs and roads of the town laid out neatly beneath us. Then we cross the Churchill River. The river is broad and shallow—most of it was hijacked long ago to feed hydroelectric dams along the Nelson River. Wide plates of glare ice are piled against the shore, but the centre of the river is open, purpled by wind and flashing in the sun. Above the tide line there's a broad swath of windboard and long, wavering lines like ellipses on the hard snow—bear tracks. Fort Prince of Wales is beneath us now, with blown snow piled up against its stone walls. The Hudson's Bay Company, as the first government in Canada, built the fort during the 1700s and used it as one of its power bases in North America. It's hard to imagine anyone overwintering in such a forbidding place. (They used to leave cannonballs in the fire until they were red-hot, then hang them in the bedrooms to blunt the cold.) Samuel Hearne, the commander of the fort, was a sort of eighteenth-century-hippie who loved the north and didn't seem to mind the harsh conditions. He had already travelled all over the Arctic with the Chipewyan Indians and even participated, unwillingly, in a surprise attack on an Inuit camp on the Coppermine River, where he watched his Chipewyan companions massacre and mutilate twenty Inuit men, women and children. That experience haunted him for the rest of his life and left him with a permanent disgust for violence.

In 1775 Hearne was appointed commander of the fort, the pride of the Hudson's Bay Company. From the air, you get a good sense of the efficacy of its design—it's a "star fort" with eleven-metre-thick walls radiating out in sharpened bastions, each one presenting not only an angled (and therefore stronger) face to enemy cannonballs but also opportunities for enfilading defensive fire. It took the Hudson's Bay Company forty years to build the fort, and it was considered impregnable, but none of that mattered with the gentle, literary Sam Hearne as its commander. When the French navy showed up in 1782, Hearne decided he didn't want to see a lot of people get killed over a few bales of beaver pelts and surrendered the fort without firing a shot. Now it sits deserted on this bleak peninsula across from Churchill, with no signs of occupation except a few bear tracks around its front gate.

After a short flight up the coast, we coast in for a landing at the snow-packed airstrip at Dymond Lake. As we climb out, a big guy in a parka and mukluks greets us. He has a heavy camera around his neck and a short-barrelled 12-gauge slung over one shoulder. His name is Dennis Fast, and he's a well-known northern nature photographer who also works here as an ecotourism guide. Flipping up our hoods, we follow Dennis to the lodge, which sits on a low rise of land about a kilometre away. It's not even Halloween yet, but it's so cold that even I, a Winnipegger, can't stop remarking on it. Describing the wind as savage would be a good start. "So, Dennis, if this is your weather at the end of October, what's it like in January?"

"It's nippy," he admits. "Sun doesn't get up until ten in the morning. Strong winds, daytime highs of about forty below."

Clomping through the snow with our mittens against our faces, we finally arrive at the lodge, where a group of German tourists are standing around the wood burner drinking hot chocolate. An aroma of fresh-baked muffins issues from the kitchen. Doug Webber appears, greets me with his customary hearty handshake and offers me a chair by the fire. A moment later his wife, Helen, comes out of the kitchen with a tray of hot muffins and coffee. They are bluff and hearty grandparents who exude the energetic sparkle of teenagers. Doug, a lean and ruddy-faced sixty-one-year-old is a walking archive of local history. He grew up a prairie farm boy and came to Churchill in 1963, when it was a refuelling depot for the Strategic Air Command. It was a critical time in world history. School kids across North America were learning to avert their eyes and "duck and cover" when the sirens went off and the inevitable nuclear weapons started air-bursting above their cities. Swept-wing B-52 bombers like the one Slim Pickens piloted in *Dr. Strangelove* were regularly lifting off from Churchill's nine-thousand-foot runway, scattering the bears with their thunderous exhaust.

Doug was posted there as a radio operator for the Royal Canadian Navy, and his job was to spy on Russian radio communications emanating from Murmansk and Archangel. "We listened to NATO warplanes and the Russians playing cat and mouse," he says. "The Brits would send flights into Russian air space, probing them for a reaction and testing their response time, and the Russians would counter with overflights into the Canadian north. It was all supposed to be hush-hush, but we knew everything about the Russian personnel, and they knew everything about us. We knew the names of their bomber captains and the atomic submarine captains, and we knew the names of their wives and their kids. We'd exchange seasonal greetings, and there was a radio operator over there named Moscow Mollie who always sent me a personal greeting on my birthday."

Doug's wife, Helen, grew up in Churchill, the daughter of a fur trader, and she sometimes rode on the dogsled with her father when he made the rounds of remote Inuit communities. After she and Doug married, they decided to get into the tourist business. They built a hut at Dymond Lake in 1967 and started bringing in goose hunters. Doug learned to fly and bought a Cessna 180. Then they built a fishing lodge at North Knife Lake. Now, forty years later, they own and operate a multi-million-dollar network of outpost camps and lodges all over the region. Like most northern outfitters, they've adopted a multifaceted survival strategy. They guide hunters for geese and caribou; they host fishermen at some camps, and take people bird and beluga-watching at others; the annual caribou migration brings in a wave of tourists, and the bears are a perennial draw. As Doug puts it, "We let the animals tell us what business we're in." Helen and fellow chef Marie Woolsey have written a series of best-selling northern cookbooks, and their daughters Jeanne and Toni have brought their own husbands into the business. "Northern tourism is constantly evolving," says Doug, "and we try to anticipate the trends and stay ahead of them." He says he wants to persuade Japanese tourists to come to Churchill and make whoopee in a snowbank. "It's a big thing in Yellowknife. They believe a child will be blessed if it's conceived under the northern lights. I'd like to convince them that our northern lights are brighter and our snow is softer than those crusty snowbanks over in the Northwest Territories."

Dymond Lake can't handle as many tourists as some of the buggy operations in Churchill, and you don't see as many bears. But it's a more upscale, higher-quality experience. "There's nothing like staying right out here on the land," says their son-in-law Mike Reimer, a handsome forty-five-year-old who runs the eco-tourism end of the family business. "Sometimes you can look right out the window here and see a polar bear," says Mike. "But generally we do a lot of walking. When you see a bear, it's up close and personal, and there's nothing like being on foot in the bear's own environment."

Their guests sleep in the cabins while Mike or Dennis or one of the other guides walks night patrol. "It's a safety issue," Mike says. "Sometimes the bears will walk right through the middle of camp, and we don't want them going into the cabins."

I kick my boots off at the entrance, where a pump-action shotgun is leaning in the corner. Mike says that if you live out here, a loaded gun is never more than a few steps away. "If you ever need one, you don't want to be running around trying to remember where you put it," he says. "It's a hassle, but safety is our number one rule and you get accustomed to it. Even when you're doing your chores, you get used to working with one hand because you're always carrying a shotgun."

Mike's sister-in-law Toni comes out of the kitchen carrying another platter of delicious muffins. She listens to the conversation for a moment, then volunteers a bear story of her own. "One day, Jeanne and I went for a walk out to the landing strip with Nelson," she says. "When you're out hiking around here, you generally do a three-hundred-and-sixty-degree rotation every twenty or thirty steps to make sure a bear isn't stalking you. We were halfway to the airstrip when I spun around and saw a full-grown eight-hundred-pound male running at us."

She shouted, and Nelson fired a warning shot—a cracker shell—over the bear's head. The bear slowed down but kept coming. The magazine of his shotgun was stuffed with the standard menu of bear deterrents—one cracker shell, two rounds of birdshot and four rifled slugs. But the cracker shell jammed in the gun, and the extractor claw tore the rim off. The empty shell was now stuck in the chamber and the gun suddenly became an expensive and ineffective baseball bat. After frantically trying to remove the jammed cartridge, he swung the gun and slammed the bear in the nose. The bear stood up, swatted Nelson to the ground and lunged at the two women. Nelson jumped to his feet and smacked the bear again, hard enough that it backed off and gave them a chance to run for the lodge. As they hurried towards safety, the bear cut ahead of them and Nelson had to fight it off again. "Nelson kept telling us to run for it," Toni says. "But we weren't going to leave him alone with the bear. It would have killed him for sure, or it would have killed one of us. Our only chance was to stay together."

Finally, they regained the safety of the lodge, where the dogs spotted the bear and chased it away. "The best weapon against a bear is a dog," interjects Mike. "I'll choose a good dog over a gun any day. Dogs don't malfunction."

Nelson says he was only slightly injured. His jacket, however, wasn't so lucky. Helen fetches it and shows it to me—a slashed-up windbreaker that looks as if it has been eaten by a lawn mower.

After finishing our muffins and coffee, we zip up our parkas, pull on mitts and hats and head out for a walk along a snow-mobile trail that angles down towards the coast and circles back towards the airstrip. There are five of us—three camera-toting German guests and Mike Reimer with his backpack, binoculars and safety gear, a pistol on his belt and a shotgun loaded with three-inch magnum slugs.

"We respect the bears and the bears respect us. Polar bears aren't aggressive towards humans in a territorial sense, the way grizzlies are. So they don't feel threatened by people walking past. Most polar bear attacks are related to predatory behaviour. If you show them you're not afraid, they'll generally move off."

It's bitterly cold out here, preposterously cold, and the wind is so strong you can lean against it. The Germans are unfazed. They nod in approval as we trudge through the bleak terrain, nudging each other and gesturing towards gnarled pieces of driftwood and other photogenic points of interest. You never know when a polar bear is going to show up, and Mike says that if one suddenly appears, we should stand in a tight group and do what he says. "I'll watch his body language," Mike says. "Most of the time, the bears don't want any trouble, but every bear is different. The other day, we came upon a bear and he bluff-charged us. He stopped, ran away, then came back and bluff-charged us again. That will happen sometimes. I'm usually not too concerned. I'll let him look us over and make up his own mind about what he wants to do."

Mike says it's a good thing we don't have kids with us. Children are bad news because they excite a polar bear's predatory instinct. When his daughter was six years old, she was playing outside, in a sturdy bear-proof chain-link enclosure. A bear spotted her, charged at full speed, hit the fence and bounced off. "She thought it was funny," he says. "We brought her inside." He adds that if there's a short person in the group, the bear will often stare at them in a creepy sort of way. "The short person is the one the bear wants. So your best bet is to keep a tight group. That makes us look bigger and more formidable than we are as individuals."

We keep hiking, but still no sign of *Ursus maritimus*. Maybe all the bears are in downtown Churchill. There's not even a track in this wind-hardened snow. The Germans have been here all week and have seen some bears at close range, but they can't tell me about it because they're bundled up with frosty scarves across their faces, and in any case it's hard to understand their broken English. We walk along the snowmobile trail for a while, seeing some Arctic hares and a snowy owl, but no bears. I can't say I'm disappointed when I notice we're circling back to the lodge, where the muffins and hot chocolate await.

The Life of Brian

For half my life, I've been hearing about a character who lives in Churchill named Brian Ladoon. Churchill is such a small town that you meet everybody who's anybody, but I've never met Ladoon. He's the town's recluse. I've heard about him in magazine articles and radio programs, and I've tried to track him down, but he doesn't have a phone and nobody seems to know where he lives. It's not that they're protecting him—a lot of people shake their heads in a vexed way if you ask where you might find him. "Brian Ladoon!?" they ask, with a sound halfway between a snort and a horse laugh. "Why in heavens would you want to talk to *him?*"

Well, I want to meet him for all kinds of reasons. For one, he allegedly has strange opinions about bears. For example, he doesn't see any problem with feeding bears and seems to think that bears and dogs get along just fine. Have you ever seen the famous, poster-sized photograph of the polar bear and the sled dog romping around and embracing like they're madly in love? That's one of Ladoon's dogs. Like Lynn Rogers, he challenges conventional thinking about bears, and local tourist outfitters, self-appointed nature experts and game wardens are uncomfortable with the fact that he is out there on the tundra, walking around and dealing with polar bears in his own way and doing whatever he pleases. In Churchill, everyone plays by the rules except Brian Ladoon.

I have other reasons I'd like to meet Brian. Every time you find something really interesting going on in Churchill, it seems to connect back to him. In the restaurants and hotels, you'll see stunning paintings on the walls—bleak Hudson Bay seascapes and barren vistas of tundra with bent spruces and scudding clouds— and they always have his signature in the bottom corner. "Yes, he's a brilliant painter," sighs the proprietor. "They're worth a lot of money, and all the tourists want to buy one, but he doesn't do it anymore. He learned how to paint as well as he could paint, and then he quit. Can you believe that?"

Several years ago I was driving through rush-hour traffic in Toronto, listening to a radio program, and they started talking about a guy in Churchill, Manitoba, who was building a stone hotel on the edge of Hudson Bay. He was cutting and hand-fitting every small slab of rock, building this enormous edifice that would eventually look like some forbidding northern palace on the edge of the bay. The radio journalist enthused that there would be no place like it in the northern world, not in Finland or Siberia or anywhere. He didn't mention the builder's name until the end of the piece, but I already knew the eccentric in question had to be Brian Ladoon.

Another time, I was walking through Churchill with a photographer who was taking pictures of cute native kids. It was a sunny late-summer day, and the town's weather-beaten main street looked like a cross between a dusty village in Mongolia and the set of *A Fistful of Dollars*. Autumn, with its influx of polar bears, was only a few weeks away, and we asked the kids what they planned to do if they ran into Nanuq while they were tearing around the outskirts of town. (Their answer was joyous: "Punch him in the nose!!") As we talked to the kids, a strikingly beautiful woman strolled past. She was wearing the sort of blue jeans you can't buy at the trading post and a Chipewyan amulet at her throat. She glanced at us as she went by, and her red hair, freckled nose and smart blue eyes made such a riveting impression that we both paused in mid-step. One of us summoned the wit to ask the obvious questions—Who the heck are you? And what are you doing in Churchill?

She told us she was a registered nurse, working at the local clinic. She lived with a local artist. Perhaps we'd heard of him—a fellow named Brian Ladoon?

Damn it, I thought, who is this guy? After twenty years of crossing his tracks, I really wanted to meet him, so after flying home from the Webber camp at Dymond Lake, I stopped into Penny Rawlings' Arctic Trading Company to see if she could help me find Brian. Penny wasn't there, but the sales girl was helpful. "Why don't you leave a note for Penny?" she suggested. "She can pass it on to Brian."

"Does she know him?"

"Yeah, he's her boyfriend."

Of course. I should have known. I left Penny a note, and the next morning the elusive Brian Ladoon rang me from the front desk of the motel. I walked down the hall. Standing there by the front desk was a wiry, ponytailed, fifty-five-year-old James Coburn type who looked as though he had been up all night

doing something illegal. He was sporting black leather motorcycle pants, a headband, wire-rimmed aviator glasses and a silvery
Lucifer goatee. Sticking out his hand, he said, "Hey, partner."

"Good to meet you. I've been trying to find you."

"I don't have a phone," he said, laughing. "I have an apartment, but it's a pigsty and I never stay there."

I asked him if I could hang around with him for a while and
talk to him about polar bears. He said he was just heading out
to feed his dogs and I was welcome to come along. A few minutes later, I was bundled up and we were heading out the door
with coffees for the road. Brian had left his truck running in the
Churchillian manner. Opening the passenger door, he swept a
pile of tools, trash and ammo boxes onto the floor. A beaten-up
Winchester shotgun with electrical tape wrapped around the stock
was leaning against the passenger seat. He jammed it into the crev-
ice between the seats and made room for me to climb in.

As we drove out of town, he told me he grew up here but
was a restless kid and wanted to see the world. When he was sixteen he snuck aboard one of the freighters moored at the docks
at the edge of town, and the crew didn't find him until they were
well on their way to the North Atlantic. He told them he wanted
to work for his passage, and they didn't have much choice. He
spent four years at sea. "I went all over the world," he said, "but I
never found a place as interesting as this."

He came back home to Churchill when he was twenty years
old and decided he was going to be a painter. He moved into a shack
out on the tundra and started teaching himself to paint. He painted
hundreds of landscapes, trying to capture the subtle, shifting colours
of the tundra, the sea and the sky. He painted at night and slept in the
daytime. "When it got dark I was too scared to sleep."

"Why?"

He laughs. "There were too many bears outside!"

He says that if a bear breaks into your cabin at night, you don't have much of a chance if you're asleep—you'd have to light the lantern, get your gun and so on. "It's too late by then." So he'd sleep in the daytime, when at least he had daylight if a bear started coming through the door. He says he loves bears, but he takes a "tough love" approach. "I don't encourage any shenanigans," he says. "I know the bears in my neighbourhood and they know me. I've plugged a few, but that's the wrong way to go. You only plug them when they give you no choice. The last one I killed, there was something wrong with it. It was extremely aggressive and it stunk really bad. It killed a couple of my dogs and ate them, and that is insane behaviour. Bears will not eat dogs because dog meat stinks. Have you ever smelled wolf meat? It stinks too. It's because they eat meat. There isn't an animal on this earth that will willingly eat another carnivore."

He quit painting when he realized he had progressed as far as he could go. "But I don't live a normal life. It's an artist sort of life. I've experimented with everything—alcohol and drugs and sex. But now my passion is the Canadian Eskimo dog.* Everybody

---

* There is confusion about the term "Eskimo" and whether it is an acceptable term. The word means "eaters of raw meat," and indeed some northerners object to it, arguing that it invokes a past in which aboriginals were treated disrespectfully by colonizing Europeans. Some northerners prefer the term "Inuit," but this too is problematic. The Inuit are only one ethnic tribe within a larger racial group. All Scots may be Celts, but not all Celts are Scottish. In the same way, all Eskimos are part of the circumpolar Eskimoan race, but not all Eskimos are Inuit. The Inupiat people of Alaska and the Yupik people of Siberia have no problem being known as eaters of raw meat, and they still call themselves "Eskimo."

wants to know about endangered bears and endangered tigers and all the rest but what about endangered dogs? There are only three indigenous breeds of dog in Canada. One is already extinct, and the Canadian Eskimo dog will go extinct too, if people don't do something."

He says the Eskimo dog is a completely different animal from the well-known Siberian husky and the Alaskan malamute. Very few southerners have ever seen a bona fide Eskimo dog because there are so few of them. In the 1950s about twenty thousand Eskimo dogs lived in the north. But in the 1960s, the snowmobile made them obsolete, and within a few decades the breed had dwindled to several hundred animals. Since then, a few devotees have managed to keep it from the brink of extinction, and Ladoon has 175 of them, the largest group in existence. Several miles south of town, he unlocks a gate and we drive along a windswept ridge. When his dogs spot him approaching in the truck, they all start to howl in a sort of insane exuberant chorus—God is here.

Most of his dogs are chained up, but some of the more dominant members of the group run free and keep an eye out for bears. Asian-eyed and powerful, they look as wild as wolves, but when Ladoon gets out of the truck and walks amongst them, they fawn and wriggle. He says about twenty bears frequent the area. This is a popular spot because a nearby peninsula projects out into Hudson Bay, offering bears a bridge out onto the new sea ice and allowing them to start their hunting season earlier. As we're walking along, he kneels to examine one dog. Two of the free ones gambol around him. I keep going, checking for bear tracks. Sure enough, about forty steps farther on, I spot a trail in the snow, footprints the size of cake plates. They look fresh.

As I'm following the tracks, a flicker of movement catches my eye. About a hundred yards ahead, a polar bear rolls up onto its haunches. It has been resting on the ground. Then another bear stands up beside it. They are enormous. Sitting up, they sniff the wind, staring at me.

Well, this is it. The moment of truth. A face-to-face encounter with a polar bear. I don't know if I should get scared now. The truck is a good two hundred yards away. Brian hasn't seemed to notice them. He's kneeling in the snow beside the dog. "Hey, Brian," I call to him in a calm voice. "We have company."

Brian stands up. "Oh sure, I know those two," he says. "They've been here for two months."

"They're huge."

"Full-grown males," he says. "Lords of the Arctic. Over a thousand pounds each."

"They're not dangerous?"

"These guys? No. I'd give them a little bird shot in the rear end if they needed it. But they're cool. They know the rules. And the dogs would attack them in a second if I gave the word."

We stand there for a long moment, studying the bears, while the bears stand there, looking at us. The dogs sit at Brian's heels, glancing up at him for the slightest indication that he wants them to engage the bears. "That's what people come to see," he says, nodding towards the bears. "Money power isn't good enough for people anymore. People are searching for spirit power. Nature is the true religion, and polar bears are your nature gods."

"How old are those bears?"

"Ten years old, at least. They've been around the block; they're old and wise. It's the young bears you have to worry about. They come over the hill like teenagers swaggering into a bar. They'll walk up and swat the dogs. They have no balance. They haven't learned yet. The older bears like hanging around here because it's prime territory. And I like having them here because they run the young ones off."

"How do these two bears get along with the dogs?"

"Pretty well, but it's random. Some bears like dogs. Others hate them. Some dogs will attack bears on sight, some will hang back; others want to make contact but they don't know how. I've seen the bears come right up and lay down with the dogs and sleep with them. It's like a slot machine. You never know what's going to happen."

"What if I was here by myself and I stumbled into these guys?"

"With no dogs? They'd get up and approach you. At that point, you'd be smart to throw a mitten down and back off."

"Then what?"

"Maybe they'd sniff it, give you enough time to back away. You don't want to run. That turns them on, gets a predatory response. You know what works the best? Peeing on the ground. That keeps them sniffing for quite a while." He laughs. "Sometimes it's not that easy trying to pee when a big bear is walking towards you."

We walk back towards the truck. The dogs are curled up with their backs to the wind. Their shaggy coats are their only shelter. He admits that leaving dogs outside in this weather might seem a little harsh to city people. He says the average winter delivers a hundred days in which the noontime high is thirty-five below zero or colder. The animal rights group PETA, which counts among its supporters Pamela Anderson and Paul McCartney, has attacked him on its website, urging civilized people everywhere to join an email campaign to force him to provide the dogs with protection from the elements. But Ladoon says they don't know what they're talking about. "What do they think the polar bears do when it's cold? These dogs have evolved over thousands of years for this weather. They're impervious to cold. A high windy ridge like this is the best place for them, or their coats get packed with ice."

He also occasionally locks horns with the wildlife officers. He feeds the dogs frozen chunks of chicken and other bulk meats, and some of his critics believe that bears are attracted by the scraps. The issue came to a head when the folk singer Sylvia Tyson was performing in Churchill and came out here with her musical group to see the bears. He says their van got stuck in the snow and a big polar bear came over to see what was going on. They were afraid to get out of the van, and the bear went to sleep a few yards away. A game warden showed up and "rescued" them and reprimanded Ladoon for putting the life of a Canadian icon at risk. He says that a while later, a helicopter appeared carrying a team of wildlife officers. They shot five large bears with tranquilizer guns and hauled them off to be relocated. With the big males out of the scene, Ladoon feared that the dog camp would be wide open to any prowling sub-adults in the area. So he stood guard all day, and when he went back to town at nightfall, a young bear came into camp and attacked the chained-up dogs. When Ladoon returned in the morning he found bodies everywhere—eleven dogs severely injured, five dead, some of them eaten. "It was like a battlefield," he says. "Dead and wounded lying all around. I wanted to go and kill the bear, but the dogs needed me."

A warden came out to tranquilize the bear responsible for the attacks, but his dart gun wouldn't work. That night the bear came back, killed three more dogs and ate one of them. The next day, Ladoon hunted down and killed a crazed-looking bear that he suspected of being rabid. The game wardens said it was his own fault and refused to test the bear for disease. "They think I'm asking for trouble, keeping my dogs out here. They'd rather I moved the dogs into town, where they could keep an eye on me and play their Big Brother role. But I know how to take care of myself. I've been dealing with bears for thirty years, a lot longer than they have, and I wish they had a little respect for other people's experience. I've worked out an arrangement with the local bears, and it works just fine as long as nobody messes with it."

* * * *

Canadian citizens are legally entitled to deal with any bear that is damaging property or threatening people. But most people in Churchill prefer to call the conservation officers, not necessarily because they believe the officers know more about bears, but because the wardens have all the necessary equipment for handling bears—the radios, trucks, tranquilizer guns, helicopters, and of course the facility known as D-20, the polar bear jail.

D-20 is on the south edge of town, a large metal Quonset building like those in which the highways department keeps snowplows. It contains rows of metal-barred cages, and when you stand outside you can hear the bears inside roaring and banging the bars. No one is allowed to enter the building, because any polar bear that gets accustomed to seeing people at close range is theoretically a more dangerous animal. The bears aren't fed either, because it wouldn't be constructive if they became too fond of the place. The wildlife officers set live traps—corrugated metal cages with trap doors—in places where bears have been causing problems, or they shoot the offending animals with tranquilizer guns and bring them here. The jail has twenty-one cells, and during the height of bear season it is often at capacity. About four new inmates arrive every day. As the bears arrive at one end of the jail for processing, other bears are being marked and measured and shipped out by helicopter at the other end. It's a struggle to keep up, but the period of incarceration allows scientists to weigh the bears and get a sense of how they are doing in terms of general health and body weight after their summer-long fast.

There are more polar bears now in western Hudson Bay than there have been in recent history, but their population may soon start declining because of global warming. Polar bears are dependent on sea ice for a hunting platform, and the shorter the winter, the less time they have to hunt seals and put on weight. Spring break-up is coming earlier every year, and according to scientific studies, the sea ice on the northern cap of the planet is shrinking by tens of thousands of square miles every year. Scientists from the National Center for Atmospheric Research say that within twenty years, the overall area of Arctic sea ice may be reduced by 80 per cent. The bears of western Hudson Bay (these bears) are the southernmost population and will be the most affected by global warming. Because Churchill is such an accessible place, these bears are also the most studied, and data collected from captured bears show that they are already being affected. On average, polar bears now weigh about eighty kilograms less than they did in 1985.

With about five per cent of the world's population, the United States produces about 25 per cent of the world's carbon dioxide, which is the primary cause of global warming (China and India are equally culpable). The U.S. government has so far been reluctant to admit that American industry has anything to do with climate change and refused to sign the Kyoto Accord. But this intransigent position took a hit in late 2006, when an environmental group called the Natural Resource Defense Council (NRDC) petitioned the government on behalf of the polar bear, arguing that well-documented statistics like those above demonstrate that the bear deserves the protection of the Endangered Species Act. In 2008 the bear was classified as endangered, and now a whole new set of laws will kick in, prohibiting any activity that might adversely affect the species. Arguably, this may mean that automobile makers, city and state utilities and large polluters like coal-burning generating plants may find themselves in court for emitting pollutants that warm the atmosphere, which in turn melt the ice upon which the polar bear depends.

This, of course, is not just about polar bears. For years the NRDC—a group of lawyers, scientists and environmental activists based in New York—has been trying to apply leverage to the United States government, and the polar bear has become the perfect fulcrum. Defining the polar bear as an endangered species would supply environmentalists with a powerful tool against large corporate polluters, and it's typical of the imaginative moves employed by the NRDC. One of its most prominent lobbyists, Robert F. Kennedy Jr., knows how to mobilize public opinion, and large corporations and governments tend to regard him and his pack of baying lawyers as their worst nightmare. Kennedy is an energetic, charismatic and principled man who, if not for the family curse, might be in position to ride a wave of political disenchantment all the way into the White House. But Kennedy's first love is the environment, a passion he says was born in boyhood, when his father, Bobby, and his uncle John F. Kennedy taught him to respect native people and wildlife and took him on cross-country trips to wild places and Indian reservations.

In 1991 I happened to be in Great Whale River in northern Quebec, when Kennedy arrived with a coterie of supporters to raise awareness of Hydro-Québec's plan to flood the river for a huge hydroelectric project. Impressed by Kennedy's obvious disdain for the American power elite that spawned him, I went to New York with Chief Matthew Mukash to attend a concert where Kennedy, Jackson Browne, Bruce Cockburn and other celebrities tried to persuade the people of New York City to pressure New York State to go back on its commitment to buy electrical power from Quebec—which was Quebec's main motivation for flooding the valley of the Great Whale River. Cowed by the groundswell of public support for the river and its small Cree community, the state cancelled its order, and the Great Whale River was saved. A few years later, Kennedy organized a similar campaign to help the Haida people stop the logging of old-growth rainforest in the Queen Charlotte Islands. The logging was halted. And in Manitoba, a place where Kennedy loves to camp and fish, a province he describes as "the largest section of pristine boreal forest in the world, unroaded and uncut," he is now joining forces with Indian bands to pressure the provincial government to stop further hydro development and dam building.

On the surface, it would seem that Kennedy and other environmentalists are fighting the good fight, supporting aboriginal groups in their fight to save Mother Nature. But in politics, nothing is ever as it seems, and there are ironies aplenty. In the case of the Great Whale River fight and its star-studded "Ban the Dam Jam" concert, skeptics pointed out that the Cree were willing to accept the $225 million that came with the James Bay Agreement, but after they took the money they were unwilling to live up to the terms of the contract they signed. Other high-profile showdowns have been criticized as being not so much about resource protection as about who would do the exploiting. When the Supreme Court of Canada widened the right of natives to catch salmon and other fish species for "food and ceremonial purposes," the redneck constituency argued that those rights would be abused. And of course they often were, by masked, rifle-toting young natives who flipped the finger to resource officers, then openly advertised and sold black-market fish to anyone with the money.

One might be forgiven for assuming that the NRDC's move to force the American government to get tough on industrial polluters would be welcomed by Canadian native people. But many natives in the Arctic are dismayed by the move to make the polar bear an endangered species, and some Inuit elders have asked the NRDC to butt out and mind its own business. Polar bear hunting is a good source of income for small communities in the Arctic. Foreign sport hunters, many of them Americans, are willing to pay thirty thousand dollars or more for the opportunity to travel by dog team and hunt bears with Inuit guides, and the Inuit regard such work as a valuable chance to market their traditional skills. If the polar bear is listed as an endangered species, it will likely limit the ability of those American clients to take their trophy bear skins back to the United States, which would remove a major motive for shooting the bears in the first place. (Few hunters bother taking bear meat back to the States, and the liver of the polar bear is poisonous.) Sixty-five-year-old David Kalluk, a village elder in Resolute Bay, says it's their land, and environmentalists can't tell them what to do on it. "These hunting traditions have been part of our culture for generations and generations," he says. "And we'll keep killing bears no matter what southerners say."

The legislation therefore puts the environmentalists in opposition to the Inuit, whom it theoretically supports. And it puts the Inuit in the equally ironic position of being on the same side as wealthy American bear hunters, at least some of whom may be in cahoots with the same energy companies that are allegedly damaging the Arctic environment that sustains them. Bears are highly evolved animals, and the issues surrounding them are just as complicated. When a young bear wanders along the Hudson Bay coast, waiting for the ice to form so it can go out on the sea and hunt seals, it's just a bear, and it lives within bear society. But it's also padding its way through a heavily mined landscape of politics, tourism, science, native rights and other complexities.

When the bears are relocated from the D-20 jail, buses arrive and hundreds of tourists watch the operation from a distant, roped-off area. Wildlife officials bring out the bears, which have been put to sleep for this operation, and load them into sling nets. Then a helicopter scoops them up and hauls them many miles north, closer to the seacoast promontories where the first ice will form. At the front door of the jail, pilots are supervising the loading process, and the conservation officers are keeping an eye on the bears for signs of wakefulness. You're supposed to stay behind the rope, but I've made some friends here, and in any case the uniforms are generally too busy to pay much attention to a stranger in their midst as long as he doesn't get in the way.

The standard inhabitant of the polar bear jail is a sub-adult—the ursine equivalent of a juvenile delinquent—and today's cast of parolees pretty much fits the norm. The first candidate weighs about two hundred kilograms. Sprawled chest down on a flatbed cart, the young male is hauled out of the jail behind an all-terrain vehicle. It may only be a sub-adult, but it is a large animal nevertheless. It has been tranquilized with a drug called Telesol, which paralyzes its muscles but allows it to remain conscious. When the drug begins to wear off, the bear first regains use of its head and neck muscles, so you need to stay away from its head. "Stay away from his head," everyone keeps calling out. It's been a busy day, choppers coming and going, so this bear has already been knocked out for a while and it's waking up. With its front legs splayed and its back legs stretched out behind it like a bulldog, it's got its head up and is watching all this activity with bewilderment and hard anger in its eyes.

The helicopter pilot, Scott de Windt, a burly guy in muddy coveralls, is carefully laying out the sling net and making sure everything is done properly. It's his job to make sure that both man and bear survive this rather dicey procedure. Alan Kristenson is a twenty-five-year-old backup pilot who's not flying today, but has transported enough bears that he can explain what's going on. "It's tricky slinging out a bear," he says. "It's much more complicated than you might think."

He says that the Jet Ranger helicopter sitting in the background can lift twelve hundred pounds and rents out for about thirteen hundred dollars per hour. They haul the bears to the North Knife River, about fifty kilometres up the coast. He says the biggest bear they ever had to move was a fifteeen-hundred-pound male. "With a load that heavy, you have to be very careful."

When the pilot arrives at the release area, he flies in a circle, making sure there are no other bears around. If you leave a tranquilized bear in the presence of other bears they might eat it. The pilot works alone—the machine can't lift another passenger—so he has to lay the bear down on a slope so that he can roll it over on its chest and make sure it has a clear airway. Sometimes the bear is awake and almost mobile by the time he parks the machine, and releasing it from the net can be touchy. "Sometimes we'll put a sub-adult in the cabin of the chopper," he says. "They glare at you while you're flying. It's pretty spooky."

As they prepare the sling net, the paralyzed bear watches them. Tilting his head from side to side, he suddenly stares at me. I'm keeping my distance ("Stay away from his head!"), but am still close enough to smell his breath. Even though the bear is temporarily paraplegic, it's an intense experience to lock eyes with the world's largest carnivore. He's panting, his jaws agape, and his breath is shooting steam in the cold air. As his eyes fix on mine, I register an involuntary twinge of fear. It's what a bird must experience when it meets the gaze of a bobcat. I've locked eyes with numbers of black bears, bad dogs and bad people, but there's something in a polar bear's gaze that burns right down into the four-million-year-old root of the human heart.

A moment later, they roll the bear off the trailer and into the net. There's a sense of urgency now as they truss him into the net. The wildlife officers don't want to tranquilize him again, and the helicopter pilot wants to get underway before the animal gets too alert. When the bear is properly cinched up, Scott de Windt climbs into the Jet Ranger and spools up the engine.

Screaming turbines, a blast of wind. The rotors change pitch and the machine teeters upwards, fetching up against the cable, which tightens and gently lifts the bear off the ground. Swaying above the load, the helicopter steadies and leans into its task. Everyone is standing, holding their mitts over their faces against the flying ice. A few seconds later the wind dies and the chopper goes drumming off towards the Barren Lands, with the pendant bear hanging beneath it on a thread.

Selected Bibliography

Epp, Henry, ed. *Three Hundred Prairie Years: Henry Kelsey's Inland Country of Good Report*. Regina, SK: Canadian Plains Research Center, 1993.

Godman, John. *American Natural History*. Philadelphia: Carey and Lea, 1826. [Available online at Google books: http://books.google.com.]

Hart, Stephen Harding and Archer Butler Hulbert, eds. *The Southwestern Journals of Zebulon Pike, 1806–1807*. Albuquerque, NM: University of New Mexico Press, 2006.

Helper, Hinton Rowan. *The Land of Gold: Reality Versus Fiction*. Baltimore: H. Taylor, 1855. [Available online through the Library of Congress's American Memory site: http://memory.loc.gov/ammem/browse.]

Herrero, Stephen. *Bear Attacks: Their Causes and Avoidance*. 1985. Reprint, Guilford, CT: Lyons Press, 2002.

Moulton, Gary E., ed. *The Definitive Journals of Lewis and Clark: From the Pacific to the Rockies*. Lincoln, NE: University of Nebraska Press, 2002. [Available online at http://lewisandclarkjournals.unl.edu/index.html.]

Olsen, Jack. *Night of the Grizzlies*. Moose, WY: Homestead Publishing, 1996.

Peacock, Doug. *Grizzly Years: In Search of the American Wilderness*. New York: Henry Holt and Company, 1996.

Ross, W. Gillies. *Arctic Whalers, Icy Seas: Narratives of the Davis Strait Whale Fishery.* Toronto: Irwin, 1985.

Seton, Ernest Thompson. *Biography of a Grizzly.* New York: Century Co., 1900.

Shelton, James Gary. *Bear Attacks: The Deadly Truth.* Hagensborg, BC: Pallister Publishing, 1998.

———. *Bear Encounter Survival Guide.* Hagensborg, BC: Pallister Publishing, 1997.

Stirling, I. *Polar Bears.* Ann Arbor, MI: University of Michigan Press, 1988.

Storer, Tracy I., and Lloyd P. Tevis, Jr. *California Grizzly.* Berkeley: University of California Press, 1955.

Teggart, Frederick J., ed. *The Portola Expedition of 1769–1770, Diary of Miguel Costanso.* Berkeley, CA: University of California Press, 1911. [A compilation of the diary is available at http:anza.uoregon.edu (archives).]